The Shirley Letters

The Shirley Letters

Being Letters written in 1851-1852 from the
California Mines

by
"Dame Shirley"
(Louise Amelia Knapp Smith Clappe)

With an Introduction by
RICHARD E. OGLESBY

Gibbs M. Smith, Inc.
Peregrine Smith Books
Salt Lake City

Seventh Printing, 1985

The Shirley Letters was first published serially
in *The Pioneer* Magazine during 1854 and 1855.

ISBN 0-87905-004-7

INTRODUCTION

According to tradition, the catalyst which sent San Franciscans scurrying to the mountains in mid-May 1848 in search of gold was the appearance of Sam Brannan, lately returned from the American River where he had been investigating rumors that the precious metal had been discovered in quantity on the property of John Sutter. The flamboyant Brannan reputedly ran through the plaza waving a bottle of dust aloft and shouting, "Gold! Gold! Gold from the American River!" Whether or not the incident took place, within hours of Brannan's return the fledgling city by the bay became a ghost town as storekeepers closed their doors, workmen dropped their tools, and even sailors left their ships to seek a fortune in the steep canyons and along the icy streams which tumbled out of the Sierra Nevada. From San Franscisco the electrifying news spread quickly southward to Monterey and Los Angeles in California, both of which suffered the same fate as San Francisco, and beyond into the Mexican provinces of Baja California and Sonora. Ships carried word of the excitement north to Oregon and across the sea to Hawaii, Australia, and the Asian mainland, as well as to the Pacific states of Central and South America, prompting a stream of gold seekers from the entire region to converge on the small strip of territory bounded by the Feather River on the north and the Tuolumne River on the south which became known as the "Mother Lode country.

The gold fever which had infected the Pacific Basin during the summer of 1848 spread in its most virulent form to the United States after President James K. Polk, in his annual message to Congress in December, gave veracity to the reports which had been circulating on the East Coast since August. Gold swiftly monopolized men's thoughts, and usually sober and sensible individuals forgot home, family, and occupation in favor of making plans to depart for gold country as soon as possible. Those who could afford it, and the 49ers were a relatively affluent lot, booked passage on anything afloat that could be pointed along the 18,000 mile route around Cape Horn to San Francisco. Others, seeking to save time, sailed for the isthmus of Panama, there to fight mosquitoes, disease, and bandits while struggling through the jungles to the Pacific, only to have to join hundreds of their impatient countrymen anxiously awaiting passage to the Golden Gate.

Though thousands eventually went to California by sea, the majority of 49ers set out overland via several routes spanning the continent. Their appetites had been whetted over the long winter by a host of speakers who took to the lecture circuits in order to describe, by means of imagination rather than information, the ease with which fortunes were to be found in the mines. The same eager audience avidly read the spate of guidebooks, some printed within days of the President's announcement, which purported to show the easiest routes to the gold fields, explained prospecting techniques to the uninitiated, and tried to sell a variety of mechanical devices "guaranteed" to find gold for their purchasers. Merchants and moneylenders did a booming business in the spring as men, heedless of the costs, outfitted themselves for the journey.

As soon as the winter moderated, hordes of argonauts took to the trails westward from Independence, Westport,

St. Joe, and other points of embarkation along the Missouri. In the first scrambles to cross the river, men fought to the death for space on the ferries, but gradually order was established, and two week waits where not uncommon. Once beyond the Missouri Valley, the travelers found that hardships increased. Cold, wet weather persisted through the spring and much of the summer of 1849, bogging down wagons, shortening tempers, and bringing disease. Asiatic cholera dogged every trail, and thousands of would be miners never reached the high plains before this dread killer put them under. Perhaps the worst difficulty was distance, for few 49ers realized the width of the continent or the nature of the country they would have to traverse. The plains, a seemingly endless expanse unbroken by trees, the towering Rockies, passable but awe inspiring with snow capped peaks visible for hundreds of miles, the deserts beyond, trailless, waterless, and wide, and, finally, the formidable Sierras, stark, steep, and troublesome to cross, barred the way to El Dorado. Late starters took a more southerly route, but with no diminution of difficulty. The Gila River path, successfully traversed by Juan Bautista de Anza three quarters of a century before, took a terrible toll, as did the aptly named Death Valley. Few, indeed, were the 49ers who did not suffer more than their share of hardships before reaching the promised land.

But the adversities of the trail were forgotten once California was reached for the wealth was there; not as much, perhaps, as promised by the guidebooks, but riches beyond a man's dreams nonetheless. Ten million dollars worth of gold came out of the mines in 1849, and that figure quadrupled the next year. Some individuals made fabulous strikes—a single prospector panned over five thousand dollars in gold along the Yuba River; two men took seventeen thousand dollars out of a single canyon—

and it mattered not that the average miner worked for little more than day wages, and quickly spent even that at the faro tables or on incredibly priced equipment and supplies. Tomorrow, each man firmly believed, would bring the big find.

Life was not idyllic in the mines, however, as the 49ers soon discovered. The simple labor of mining, whether alone or in company with one or more partners, was bone hard. From dawn to dusk the prospector was knee and elbow deep in icy water, washing out pan after pan of gold bearing sand and gravel. Working a sluice box or cradle meant moving several tons of dirt per day with pick and shovel, though it was usually more productive than panning. Home generally was a blanket thrown down on the claim, or, at best, a tent, for few miners could afford the rent charged in the rooming houses which sprang up in the larger camps. Wind and rain hampered operations, and, much to the dismay of the 49ers, who had spent months struggling to get to California, the mining season was closed from the first heavy rains of the autumn until after the flooding runoff of winter snows in the spring. During that space of time, the miner had to leave the diggings, repair to one of the valley cities, Sacramento or Stockton, or to San Francisco to seek some form of livelihood until he could return to the mountains. Add to that the dreary daily diet of pork and beans, with little of the former and much of the latter, and the life of a miner was pretty grim.

Yet there was a romantic air about the mines which lasted pretty generally down to the end of the 1852 season. The miners, each a scraggly-faced stereotype of a frontiersman, ragged, dirty, run down at the heels, equipped with a blanket or two, knife, pistol, mining tools, and a modicum of cookware, were ever ready to run to a new location on the merest mention of a rumored strike, carefree, happy-go-lucky, secure in the knowledge that they were only temporarily in California, and that as soon as they made their pile, they would be off for the States. In those flush early years, Americans were usually too busy to notice whether their neighbors were white, black, brown, yellow, red, or any of the indeterminate shades which appeared, and cared little whether the miner panning the adjacent claim was God-fearing or one of those "assassins manufactured in Hell." The prospector hurried constantly onward following the main chance, a willing participant in one of mankind's greatest adventures.

And it was, literally, mankind which participated in the gold rush, for woman kind, at least of the "proper" variety, was almost totally absent. The first census of 1850 indicated that the population of California was over ninety percent male, and the state count two years later showed little change. In the absence of this ameliorating influence, "Human character crumbled and vanished like dead leaves," at least according to observer Clarence King. But though women were indeed few, and miners would later reckon the coming of civilization from the arrival of the first "nice" women, posterity has reason to be glad for the appearance in the mountains of one of the finest ladies ever to grace the Golden State by her presence, Mrs. Louisa Amelia Knapp Smith Clapp.

Mrs. Clapp, or as she will forever be affectionately known to Californians, Dame Shirley, came to California, via Cape Horn, in 1849, following a whim of her fiddle-footed husband. After a stay in San Francisco, where he suffered from the fogs and bilious fevers of the bay area, Fayette Clapp, himself a doctor, left his wife behind and journeyed far up the Feather River, hoping that the crisp, clean air of the mountains would have a salubrious effect on his health, and that the demand for medical men in the wilderness would have a similar impact on his income. Clapp's health improved markedly over the summer of

1851, though the same could not be said for his finances due to the presence of twenty-nine doctors in Rich Bar, and he invited Shirley to join him at the bustling camp high on the East Fork of the Feather that fall. She remained at Rich Bar, and nearby Indian Bar, until the end of the 1852 season, and from those addresses penned a series of twenty-three letters to her sister back home in Massachusetts, letters which have become classics in gold rush literature. That this tiny, not very robust, proper New England lady could have survived in a primitive mining camp, let alone produce there a masterpiece of literature and history, is one of those miracles for which subsequent generations will ever be grateful.

Louisa Amelia Knapp Smith was born in Elizabeth, New Jersey, in or about the year 1819. Orphaned at an early age, her father died in 1832 and her mother in 1837, she nonetheless had the wherewithal, and the support of a conscientious guardian, to obtain a good formal education. She attended the "Female Seminary" in Charlestown, Massachusetts, in 1837, and Amherst Academy the following two years. Much of her time there was spent learning all those horrible ways to murder the English language then in vogue in preparation for a possible career in letters. Louisa Smith's writing proclivities were strengthened through a chance meeting, while traveling on a stagecoach, with Alexander Hill Everett, noted diplomat, author, orator, though not so famous in this field as his brother, Edward, and editor of the *North American Review*. Charmed by the lovely young student, Everett immediately took a great interest in her development as a writer.

It is difficult to determine whether Everett's encouragement was due to a belief that Louisa Smith had in her a spark of creative genius, or was the result of the fact that he had fallen hopelessly in love with her. Considering himself a suitor, even though twice her age, Everett kept up a voluminous correspondence which terminated only with his death in 1847. While Louisa rejected her distinguished friend as a lover, she doted on his repeated advice and assurance. He continually adjured her to read widely and write constantly, and even managed to secure publication of one of Louisa's poems in the *United States Magazine and Democratic Review* in 1844. It is doubtful if the American reading public deserved such an infliction, but it was a tonic for Louisa, kept her literary interest active, and gave her the confidence necessary for aspiring authors.

Everett's heart was broken, or perhaps it was only his pride which was wounded, when Louisa wrote to him announcing her engagement to young Fayette Clapp, a Massachusetts native five years her junior. Everett, then serving on a diplomatic mission out of the country, asked, or rather, demanded, information concerning his successful rival, and must have been disappointed in Louisa's choice, for her fiance had little distinguishing about him at the time. Born into a large family, Clapp had done a variety of things, including clerking in a store, before attending Princeton and Brown universities. At one point he decided to become a minister, and had gone so far as to enroll in the Williston Academy, Easthampton, Massachusetts, but that interest waned. After his graduation from Brown, Clapp took up the study of medicine in the office of a relative, Sylvanus Clapp, and was intrigued enough to matriculate at Castleton Medical College in Vermont for formal training. It was during this time that he met and married Louisa Smith, and, before he could complete his regular medical education, gold fever attacked him. With Louisa in tow, Fayette Clapp left New England for the gold fields of California.

That is not to say that Louisa Clapp went against her

will, for she loved to travel. "I fancy that Nature intended me for an Arab or some other nomadic barbarian," she wrote her stay-at-home sister, Mary Jane, in an attempt to explain to her the sudden departure, and to convey some of the sense of excitement and adventure that were part of her California excursion. Shirley must have been speaking the truth, for assuredly she was willing to tolerate a great deal of discomfort to satisfy that wanderlust.

San Francisco in 1849 and 1850 must have been a distinct shock to the new arrivals after the staid, regular existence of long settled Massachusetts. Few of the essentials and none of the amenities were available in that ant hill of frenzied existence. The "city" was little more than a rambling tent and shack town sprawled over the hills and into the valleys stretching back from the bustling waterfront, windswept, dusty and muddy by turns, and hopping with fleas. A sign posted at the corner of Clay and Kearney Streets, where the wood frame Parker House was rising in 1849, epitomized the condition of municipal improvements—"This Street is Impassable, Not Even Jackassable." During wet weather, drunks who fell from the board sidewalks into the streets were known to drown before help could reach them. Yet there was a contagious excitement about the place, an anticipation of wealth and greatness to come which affected even those most re pelled by its physical condition.

San Francisco was a true boom town, and commodities were priced accordingly. Bread, for which Shirley had paid four or five cents a loaf back East, sold for from fifty to seventy-five cents a loaf in San Franicsco. Eastern newspapers, no matter what their vintage, were worth a dollar per paper. The smallest coin in circulation was the quarter, and merchants did little actual selling in their stores. Customers either bought at the posted prices, however exorbitant, or did without. The population expanded daily. From a hamlet of 812 in the spring of 1848, to a town of 5,000 in the summer of 1849, to a full-fledged city of 25,000 by mid-1850, San Francisco burgeoned, and the variety of people walking her streets was amazing. Yankees and Californios, Chinese and Chileans, Sydney Ducks and Kanakas all rubbed elbows, and only occasionally struck sparks. Saloons, brothels, and gambling halls abounded, providing entertainment for young men, far from home, lonely, and in need of constant excitement to draw their attention from the incredible hardships and almost uniform lack of success they experienced.

Such an unfolding panorama provided a wealth of subjects for a perceptive author, and, while her husband cast about, rather unsuccessfully, for a means of livelihood, Shirley practiced her art. Some of her sketches and poems were published in the Marysville *Herald* in the spring and summer of 1851, but they retained the florid, unnatural style of the period, and would now rest in appropriate obscurity had not their author later become famous. What purged her writing of its designed artificiality and elevated it into immortal purity in the few weeks between the appearance of her last effort in the *Herald* and her first letter from Rich Bar? No one can say for sure, but two things perhaps contributed.

The breathtaking beauty of the mountains had an obvious impact. "I wish I could give you some faint idea of the majestic solitudes through which we passed," Shirley wrote of her trip to Rich Bar, and her first glimpse of the camp's site from high on the edge of the canyon moved her to comment, "Deep in the shadowy nooks of the far down valleys, like wasted jewels dropped from the radiant sky above, lay half a dozen blue-bosomed lagoons, glittering and gleaming and sparkling in the sunlight, as though each tiny wavelet were formed of rifted diamonds. It was worth the whole wearisome journey . . . to behold this beautiful vision." Such country needed no contrived embellishment from the author.

Society in Rich Bar itself, so startlingly different from Amherst in its masculinity, mobility, and freedom also must have been impressive. There was little in Shirley's background to permit any comparison, and the freshness and newness of everything, the astonishing paradoxes—the opulent gambling parlor of the Empire next to the hovels of the miners, the luxury of brandied fruit against wormy flour—seemed to elicit a sensitivity on Shirley's part not previously apparent in her writing. The presence of large quantities of money, too, made her aware of some of the fundamental drives of man, and the sympathy and understanding evoked from her by that awareness needed no manufactured means of expression.

Rich Bar, as a mining camp, was aptly named. Discovered in the summer of 1850 by gold hunters straggling home from the ill-fated "Gold Lake" search, Rich Bar sprang into almost instantaneous being when a prospector by the name of Greenwood washed nearly three thousand dollars out of two pans excavated on the site. Hundreds of others flocked to the location, and so productive were the diggings that a limit of ten square feet was established as the maximum size of a claim. In the first flush months, when men were busy burrowing into the banks and bed of the stream, little attention was paid to the establishment of a permanent camp. Supplies and equipment had to be brought in by pack mule over the single steep trail winding up the East Fork of the Feather. The summer of 1851, however, brought a throng to Rich Bar, storekeepers, gamblers, doctors, and others besides miners who saw in the valuable strike some sort of opportunity for themselves. While the miners constructed wing dams, flumes, and other works, the Empire Saloon and Rooming House, several store buildings, and even a few log dwellings were built as the place took on an air of permanence. Merchants, including the brother of future California historian Hubert H. Bancroft, did a brisk business as gold production was excellent. Rich Bar would produce between three and four million dollars in gold during its brief existence.

But the story of Rich Bar and environs is not the story of gold extraction or the meteoric rise and decline of a mining camp. It is the story of diverse peoples thrown together in a special situation, their interactions, and the insights they provide into the nature of the human animal and the workings of California and American History. This is the tale that Shirley incomparably tells. Driven by an insatiable curiosity and blessed with superb powers of observation, the little New England woman faithfully recorded what she saw, and accurately described everything from mining techniques to the drinking habits of miners. In so doing, she has provided posterity with the human side of the mining frontier, and a glimpse of the personal lives of the miners which is available in no other source.

Shirley got a good, long look at "that most piquant specimen of brute creation, the California 'Elephant.' " Nothing about the beast escaped her probing eye, nothing was left out of her detailed descriptions. At one point she wrote, "In the short space of twenty-four days, we have had murders, fearful accidents, bloody deaths, a mob, whippings, a hanging, an attempt at suicide, and a fatal duel." This was certainly enough to intimidate the strongest woman, but proved barely sufficient to provide fuel for a single letter. She obviously did not "leave out the darker shades of . . . mountain life," as so many commentators on the mines tended to do, and, moreover, was able to point out various reasons for some of the more blatant violations of civilized behavior, such as the three week Christmas binge engaged in by the miners. She also wit-

nessed the beginning manifestations of the racial antagon-
isms harbored by her fellow Americans that last summer,
and did not hesitate to register her disgust at the treatment meted out to Mexicans, Negroes, and others who
seemed "different." "Their Majesties the Mob" held no
charms for her, even though she left the mines before
racism and vigilante justice became the rule rather than
the exception.

Though the horrible was ever present, and perhaps as
the wife of a physician she got to see more of it than usual,
Shirley did not neglect the beautiful and elevating. Her
descriptions of the river, the countryside, and the climate
are a Chamber of Commerce man's dream—"The day was
beautiful; but when is it ever otherwise in the mountains
of California?"—and provide an almost photographic view
of the mountain country in 1851 and 1852. Meals in the
diggings could be just as magnificent as the scenery, as her
description of a breakfast at the home of a friend indi-
cates, but starving times were just as common, when
oysters, salmon, beef, champagne, and milk were only vi-
sions from a dim and distant past.

But the major business of the East Fork was mining,
and Shirley not only observed the miners at work, but actually tried her hand at it, becoming "a *mineress*." In the
process, she became painfully aware of the drawbacks of
the profession, writing, "I can truly say . . . 'I am sorry I
learned the Trade,' for I wet my feet, tore my dress, spoilt
a new pair of gloves, nearly froze my fingers, got an awful
headache, took cold and lost a valuable breastpin, in this
my labor of love." Her reward for such toil was a munifi-
cent three dollars and twenty-five cents. That experience,
she well knew, was not atypical, for while "lucky strikes"
did occur on rare occasions, Shirley was "acquainted with
many . . . whose gains have *never* amounted to much
more than 'wages;' that is, from six to eight dollars a day."

This was particularly true in 1852, when the miners put forth an all out effort in the summer, damming, fluming, and coyoting in an effort to reach bed rock. They did it, and found nothing there. Discouraged and defeated, they left the East Fork in large numbers, with the Clapps, waiting until almost too late, following them out, never to return.

It was not a happy leave taking for Shirley, and her lament on that occasion provides a clue to the sensitivity of her epistles. "I *like* this wild and barbarous life; I leave it with regret. Here, at least, I have been contented." It is this love for the rough life and those who shared it with her that shines through her letters.

The Clapps went back to San Francisco where their marriage dissolved. Fayette went on to Hawaii and a variety of other places, never looking back. Shirley stayed in San Francisco, divorcing her husband eventually, and became one of the city's most beloved schoolteachers. She continued her interest in the literary world, and met Ferdinand Ewer, the founder of *The Pioneer*, a short-lived periodical out of San Francisco. Ewer apparently saw copies of Shirley's letters, immediately perceived their worth, and every issue of *The Pioneer*, from its inception, January, 1854, to its demise in December, 1855, contained one of them. From that ephemeral publication they were picked up by Josiah Royce, Hubert H. Bancroft, and other historians who heaped lavish praise on them and insured their immortality. Bret Harte borrowed heavily from Shirley's descriptions of mining life, and two of his classic stories, "The Outcasts of Poker Flat" and "The Luck of Roaring Camp," were taken directly from incidents portrayed in the Letters. Even Mark Twain may have been inspired by Shirley's description of a tame frog to create his "Celebrated Jumping Frog of Calaveras

County." In any case, her letters were read and appreciated, even at the time.

After a generation of teaching, Shirley was forced to retire because of ill health in 1878. She left San Francisco and returned east to be with her niece in New York. Finally, she moved out to Overbrook Farm, a retirement home run by relatives of Bret Harte near her birthplace in New Jersey, where she died in 1906. Shirley was buried as "Louise Clappe, wife of Dr. Fayette Clappe," as perhaps a nostalgic remembrance of those glorious days in California, where she had been content.

In 1922, Thomas Russell put Shirley's letters together in book form, adding to them an "Appreciation" by one of her former students. Eleven years later the late Carl I. Wheat edited them, with additional information about their author, for the Grabhorn Press in San Francisco, an edition which Alfred A. Knopf reprinted in popular format in 1949. But all of these editions are now rare, and Shirley has been denied to the general reader. Rodman W. Paul, in his excellent article, "In Search of Dame Shirley," *Pacific Historical Review*, XXXIII, No. 2 (May, 1964), 127-146, brought together all the known information about the little New England schoolteacher, but not even he could explain how her letters came to be addressed to all readers at all times. But explanations are not really necessary. The letters are ours to profit from, and ours to enjoy. For that we shall always be grateful to Dame Shirley.

Richard E. Oglesby
University of California
Santa Barbara

CONTENTS

CONTENTS

The Shirley Letters

". . . a series of letters, written by a lady who came to California in 1849, to her sister in 'the States,' as the land we left behind us was called at that time. They are penned in that light, graceful, epistolary style, which only a lady can fall into; and as they are a transcript of the impressions which the condition of California affairs, two years ago, made upon a cultivated mind, cannot fail to be of general interest."

THE PIONEER
January, 1854

LETTER FIRST

A TRIP INTO THE MINES

Rich Bar,
East Branch of the North Fork of Feather River,
September 13, 1851

I CAN easily imagine, dear M——, the look of large wonder, which gleams from your astonished eyes, when they fall upon the date of this letter. I can figure to myself your whole surprised attitude, as you exclaim, "What in the name of all that is restless, has sent 'Dame Shirley' to Rich Bar? How did such a shivering, frail, home-loving little thistle ever float safely to that far away spot, and take root so kindly, as it evidently has, in that barbarous soil? Where in this living, breathing world of ours, lieth that same Rich Bar, which, sooth to say, hath a most taking name? And for pity's sake how does the poor little fool expect to amuse herself there?"

Patience, sister of mine. Your curiosity is truly laudable; and I trust that before you read the postscript of this epistle, it will be fully and completely relieved. And first, I will merely observe *en passant*—reserving a full description of its discovery for a future letter—that said Bar forms a part of a mining settlement situated on the East Branch of the North Fork of Feather River, "away off up in the mountains," as our "little Faresoul" would say, at almost the highest point where, as yet, gold has been dis-

1

covered, and indeed, within fifty miles of the summit of
the Sierra Nevada itself. So much at present, for our *locale*, while I proceed to tell you of the propitious—or un-
propitious as the result will prove—winds, which blew us
hitherward.

You already know, that F——, after suffering for an entire year, with fever and ague, bilious, remittent, and in-
termittent fevers—this delightful list, varied by an occa-
sional attack of jaundice,—was advised as a *dernier resort*
to go into the mountains. A friend, who had just returned
from the place, suggested Rich Bar, as the terminus of his
health-seeking journey; not only on account of the extreme purity of the atmosphere, but because there were
more than a thousand people there already, and but one
physician; and as his strength increased, he might find in
that vicinity a favorable opening for the practice of his
profession, which, as the health of his purse was almost as
feeble as that of his body, was not a bad idea.

F—— was just recovering from a brain fever, when he
concluded to go to the mines; but in spite of his excessive
debility, which rendered him liable to chills at any hour of
the day or night, he started on the seventh day of June—
mounted on a mule, and accompanied by a jackass to
carry his baggage, and a friend, who kindly volunteered to
assist him in spending his money—for this wildly beautiful
spot. F—— was compelled by sickness to stop several days
on the road. He suffered immensely; the trail for many
miles, being covered to the depth of twelve feet with
snow, although it was almost midsummer when he passed
over it. He arrived at Rich Bar the latter part of June, and
found the revivifying effect of its bracing atmosphere far
surpassing his most sanguine hopes. He soon built himself
an office, which was a perfect marvel to the miners, from
its superior elegance. It is the only one on the Bar, and I

intend to visit it in a day or two, when I will give you a description of its architectural splendors. It will perhaps enlighten you as to one peculiarity of a newly discovered mining district, when I inform you that although there were but two or three physicians at Rich Bar when my husband arrived, in less than three weeks there were *twenty-nine* who had chosen this place for the express purpose of practising their profession.

Finding his health so almost miraculously improved, F—— concluded, should I approve the plan, to spend the winter in the mountains. I had teased him to let me accompany him when he left in June; but he had at that time refused, not daring to subject me to inconveniences, of the extent of which he was himself ignorant. When the letter disclosing his plans for the winter reached me at San Francisco, I was perfectly enchanted. You know that I am a regular Nomad in my passion for wandering. Of course my numerous acquaintances in San Francisco raised one universal shout of disapprobation. Some said that I ought to be put into a strait jacket, for I was undoubtedly mad to think of such a thing. Some said that I should never get there alive, and if I *did*, would not stay a month; and others sagely observed—with a profound knowledge of the habits and customs of the aborigines of California— that even if the Indians *did not* kill me, I should expire of *ennui* or the cold before spring. One lady declared in a burst of outraged modesty, that it was absolutely indelicate, to think of living in such a large population of men; where at the most there were but two or three women. I laughed merrily at their mournful prognostications, and started gaily for Marysville, where I arrived in a couple of days ready to commence my journey to Rich Bar. By the way, I may as well begin the chapter of accidents which distinguished it, by recounting our mule ride from a

Ranch ten miles distant from Marysville, where, as I had spent part of the summer, the larger portion of my wardrobe still remained. We had stopped there for one night to enable me to arrange my trunks for the journey.

You have no idea of the hand to mouth sort of style in which most men in this country are in the habit of living. Of course, as usual with them, the person who had charge of the house, was out of provisions when we arrived. Luckily I had dined a couple of stages back, and as we intended to leave on the following day for Marysville, I did not mind the scanty fare. The next morning friend P—— contrived to gather together three or four dried biscuits, several slices of hard, salt ham and some poisonous green tea, upon which we breakfasted. Unfortunately, a man, whom F—— was expecting on important business, did not arrive until nearly night, so I had the pleasure of sitting half the day, robed, hatted and gauntleted for my ride. Poor P—— had been deep in the mysteries of the severest kind of an ague since ten o'clock, and as we had swept the house of everything in the form of bread early in the morning, and nothing remained but the aforesaid ham, it was impossible to procure any refreshment.

About half an hour before sunset, having taken an affecting farewell of the turkeys, the geese, my darling chickens, about eighty in number, to nearly every one of which I had given an appropriate name, the dog, a horrid little imp of a monkey, poor P—— *and* his pet ague, we started merrily for Marysville, intending to arrive there about supper time. But as has been said at *least* a thousand times before, "man proposes and God disposes," for scarcely had we lost sight of the house, when all of a sudden, I found myself lying about two feet deep in the dust, my saddle, being too large for the mule, having turned and deposited me on that safe but disagreeable couch. F—— of

course was sadly frightened, but as soon as I could clear
my mouth and throat from dirt—which filled eyes, nose,
ears and hair—not being in the least hurt, I began to laugh
like a silly child; which had the happy effect of quite reas-
suring my good *sposo*. But such a looking object as I was, I
am sure you never saw. It was impossible to recognize the
original color of habit, hat, boots or gloves. F—— wished
me to go back, put on clean clothes and make a fresh start;
but you know M——, that when I make up my *mind* to it, I
can be as wilful as the gentlest of my sex; so I decidedly
refused, and, the road being *very* lonely, I pulled my veil
over my face, and we jogged merrily onward, with but
little fear of shocking the sensibilities of passing travellers
by my strange appearance.

As F—— feared another edition of my downfall, he
would not allow the mules to canter or trot, so they
walked all the way to Marysville where we arrived at midnight. There we came within an ace of experiencing number two of the 'accidents,' by taking our *nunc dimittis* in
the form of a death by starvation. We had not eaten since
breakfast, and as the fires were all extinguished, and the
servants had retired at the hotel, we of course could get
nothing very nourishing *there*. I had no idea of regaling
my fainting stomach upon pie and cheese, *even* including
those tempting and saw-dustiest of luxuries, *crackers!* So
F——, dear soul, went to a restaurant and ordered a *petit
souper* to be sent to our room. Hot oysters, toast, toma-
toes and coffee—the only nourishment procurable at that
hour of the night—restored my strength, now nearly exhausted, by want of food, falling from my mule and sitting for so many hours in the saddle.

The next morning, F—— was taken seriously ill with
one of his bilious attacks, and did not leave his bed until
the following Saturday, when he started for Bidwell's Bar,

a rag city about thirty-nine miles from Marysville, taking both the mules with him, and leaving me to follow in the stage. He made this arrangement, because he thought it would be easier for me, than riding the entire way.

On Monday the eighth of September, I seated myself in the most excruciatingly springless wagon that it was ever my lot to be victimized in, and commenced my journey in earnest. I was the only passenger. For thirty miles the road passed through as beautiful a country as I had ever seen. Dotted here and there with the California oak, it reminded me of the peaceful apple orchards and smiling river meadows of dear old New England. As a frame to the graceful picture, on one side rose the Buttes, that group of hills so piquant and saucy; and on the other tossing to Heaven the everlasting whiteness of their snow wreathed foreheads, stood, sublime in their very monotony, the glorious Sierra Nevada.

We passed one place where a number of Indian women were gathering flower-seeds, which, mixed with pounded acorns and grasshoppers, forms the bread of these miserable people. The idea, and the really ingenious mode of carrying it out, struck me as so singular, that I cannot forbear attempting a description. These poor creatures were entirely naked with the exception of a quantity of grass bound round the waist and covering the thighs midway to the knees perhaps. Each one carried two brown baskets, (which, I have since been told, are made of a species of osier,) woven with a neatness which is absolutely marvellous, when one considers that they are the handiwork of such degraded wretches. Shaped like a cone, they are about six feet in circumference at the opening, and I should judge them to be nearly three feet in depth. It is evident by the grace and care with which they handle them, that they are exceedingly light. It is possible that my description may be inaccurate, for I have never read any account of them, and merely give my own impressions as they were received, while the wagon rolled rapidly by the spot at which the women were at work. One of these queer baskets is suspended from the back and is kept in place by a thong of leather passing across the forehead. The other they carry in the right hand, and wave over the flower seeds, first to the right and back again to the left alternately, as they walk slowly along, with a motion as regular and monotonous as that of a mower. When they have collected a handful of the seeds, they pour them into the basket behind, and continue this work until they have filled the latter with their strange harvest. The seeds thus gathered are carried to their *rancherias* and stowed away with great care for winter use. It was, to me, very interesting to watch their regular motion, they seemed so exactly to keep time with each other; and with their dark shining skins, beautiful limbs and lithe forms, they were by no means the least picturesque feature of the landscape.

Ten miles this side of Bidwell's Bar, the road, hitherto so smooth and level, became stony and hilly. For more than a mile we drove along the edge of a precipice, and so near, that it seemed to me, should the horses deviate a hair's breadth from their usual track, we must be dashed into eternity. Wonderful to relate, I did not oh! nor ah! nor shriek *once*; but remained crouched in the back of the wagon as silent as death. When we were again in safety, the driver exclaimed in the classic *patois* of New England, "Wall, I guess yer the fust woman that ever rode over that are hill without hollering." He evidently did not know that it was the intensity of my *fear* that kept me so still.

Soon Table Mountain became visible, extended like an immense dining board for the giants, its summit, a perfectly straight line pencilled for more than a league against the flowing sky. And now we found ourselves among the Red Hills, which look like an ascending sea of crimson waves, each crest foaming higher and higher, as we creep among them, until we drop down suddenly, into the pretty little valley called Bidwell's Bar.

I arrived there at three o'clock in the evening where I found F—— in much better health than when he left Marysville. As there was nothing to sleep *in* but a tent, and nothing to sleep *on* but the ground, and the air was black with fleas hopping about in every direction, we concluded to ride forward to the Berry Creek House, a ranch ten miles farther on our way, where we proposed to pass the night.

The moon was just rising as we started. The air made one think of fairy festivals; of living in the woods *always* with the green-coated people for playmates, it was so wonderfully soft and cool, without the least particle of dampness. A midsummer's night in the leafy month of June, amid the dreamiest haunts of "Old Cronest," could not be more enchantingly lovely.

We sped merrily onward until nine o'clock, making the old woods echo with song and story and laughter, for F—— was unusually gay, and I was in "tip-top" spirits; it seemed to me so *funny*, that we two people should be riding on mules all by ourselves in these glorious latitudes, night smiling down so kindly upon us; and funniest of *all* that we were going to live in the Mines! In spite of my gayety however, I now began to wonder why we did not arrive at our intended lodgings. F—— re-assured me by saying that when we had *de*scended this hill or *as*cended that, we should certainly be there. But ten o'clock came; eleven, twelve, one, *two!* but no Berry Creek House! I began to be frightened; and besides that, was very sick with a nervous headache. At every step we were getting higher and higher into the mountains, and even F—— was at last compelled to acknowledge that we were *lost!* We were on an Indian trail, and the bushes grew so low, that at almost every step, I was obliged to bend my forehead to my mule's neck. This increased the pain in my head to an almost insupportable degree. At last I told F—— that I could not remain in the saddle a moment longer. Of course there was nothing to do but to camp;—totally unprepared for such a catastrophe, we had nothing but the blankets of our mules, and a thin quilt, in which I had rolled some articles necessary for the journey, because it was easier to pack than a traveling bag. F—— told me to sit on the mule while he prepared my woodland couch; but I was too nervous for that, and so jumped off and dropped on to the ground worn out with fatigue and pain. The night was still dreamily beautiful, and I should have been enchanted with the adventure, (for I had fretted and complained a good deal because we had no *excuse* for camping out,) had it not been for that impertinent headache which you remember, always *would* visit me at the most inconvenient seasons.

About daylight, somewhat refreshed, we again mounted our mules, confidently believing that an hour's ride would bring us to the Berry Creek House; as we supposed of course, that we had camped in its immediate vicinity. We tried more than a dozen paths, which, as they led *nowhere*, we would retrace to the principal trail. At last F—— determined to keep upon one, as it *must* he thought in *time*, lead us out of the mountains, even if we landed on the other side of California. Well, we rode on, and on, and on; up hill and down hill, down hill and up; through fir groves, and oak clumps, and along the edge of dark ravines, until I thought that I should go *mad*, for all this time the sun was pouring down its hottest rays most pitilessly, and I had an excruciating pain in my head and all my limbs.

About two o'clock we struck the main trail, and meeting a man,—the first human being that we had seen since we left Bidwell's—were told that we were seven miles from the Berry Creek House, and that we had been down to the North Fork of the American River, more than thirty miles out of our way! This joyful news gave us fresh strength, and we rode on as fast as our worn out mules could go.

Although we had eaten nothing since noon the day before, I bore up bravely until we arrived within two miles of the Ranch, when courage and strength both gave way, and I *implored* F——to let me lie down under a tree and rest for a few hours. He very wisely refused, knowing that if I dismounted, it would be impossible to get me on to my mule again, and we should be obliged to spend another night under the stars, which in this enchanting climate, would have been delightful, had we possessed any food. But knowing that I needed refreshment, even more than I did rest, he was compelled to insist upon my proceeding.

My poor husband! He must have had a trying time with me, for I sobbed and cried like the veriest child, and repeatedly declared that I should never live to get to the *rancho*. F—— said afterward that he began to think I intended to keep my word, for I certainly *looked* like a dying person.

Oh Mary! it makes me *shudder* when I think of the mad joy with which I saw that *rancho*! Remember that with the exception of three or four hours the night before, we had been in the saddle for nearly twenty-four hours, without refreshment. When we stopped, F—— carried me into the house and laid me on to a bunk, though I have no remembrance of it, and he said, that when he offered me

some food, I turned from it with disgust, exclaiming, "Oh
take it away; give me some cold water and let me *sleep*,
and be sure you don't wake me for the next three weeks."
And I *did* sleep with a forty slumber power; and when
F—— came to me late in the evening with some tea and
toast, I awoke—oh! *so* refreshed,—and perfectly well, for
after all the great fuss which I had made, there was nothing the matter with me but a little fatigue.

Every one that we met, congratulated us, upon not
having encountered any Indians; for the paths which we
followed were Indian trails, and it is said, they would have
killed us for our mules and clothes. A few weeks ago, a
Frenchman and his wife were murdered by them. I had
thought of the circumstances when we camped, but was
too sick to care what happened. They generally take
women captive, however, and who knows how narrowly I
escaped becoming an Indian chieftainess, and feeding for
the rest of my life upon roasted grasshoppers, acorns, and
flower-seeds? By the way, the last mentioned article of
food, strikes me as rather *poetical* than otherwise.

After a good night's rest, we are perfectly well, and as
happy as the day itself—which was one of Heaven's own
choosing—and rode to the Wild Yankee's, where we breakfasted, and had, among other dainties, fresh butter and
cream.

Soon after we alighted, a *herd* of Indians, consisting of
about a dozen men and squaws, with an unknown quantity of pappooses, the last, naked as the day they were
born, crowded into the room to stare at us. It was the
most amusing thing in the world, to see them finger my
gloves, whip, and hat, in their intense curiosity. One of
them had caught the following line of a song, "Oh! carry
me back to old Martinez," with which he continued to

stun our ears all the time we remained; repeating it over and over, with as much pride and joy, as a mocking bird will exhibit when he has learned a new sound.

On this occasion, I was more than ever struck, with what I have often remarked before, the extreme beauty of the *limbs* of the Indian women of California. Though for haggardness of expression, and ugliness of feature, they might have been taken for a band of Macbethian witches, a bronze statue of Cleopatra herself, never folded more beautifully rounded arms above its dusky bosom, or poised upon its pedestal, a slenderer ankle, or a more sta- tuesque foot, than those which gleamed from beneath the dirty blankets of these wretched creatures. There was one exception, however, to the general hideousness of their faces. A girl of sixteen perhaps; with those large, magnifi- cently lustrous, yet at the same time, soft eyes, so com- mon in novels, so rare in real life, had shyly glided, like a dark, beautiful spirit into the corner of the room. A fringe of silken jet swept heavily upward from her dusky cheek, athwart which, the richest color came and went like flashes of lightning. Her flexible lips curved slightly away from teeth like strips of cocoa-nut meat, with a mocking grace infinitely bewitching. She wore a cotton chemise, disgustingly dirty, I must confess, girt about her slender waist with a crimson handerchief; while over her night black hair, carelessly knotted beneath the rounded chin, was a purple scarf of knotted silk. Her whole appearance was picturesque in the extreme. She sat upon the ground, with her pretty, brown fingers languidly interlaced above her knee "round as a *period*," (as a certain American poet has so funnily said of a similar limb in his Diana,) and smiled up into my face, as if we were the dearest friends.

I was perfectly enraptured with this wild-wood Cleo- patra; and bored F. almost beyond endurance with exclamations about her starry eyes, her chiselled limbs, and her beautiful nut-brown cheeks.

I happened to take out of my pocket a paper of pins when all the women begged for some of them. This lovely child still remained silent in the posture of exquisite grace which she had so unconsciously assumed, but nevertheless, she looked as pleased as any of them, when I gave her also a row of the much coveted treasures. But I found I had got myself into business; for all the men wanted pins too; and I distributed the entire contents of the papers, which I happened to have in my pocket, before they were satisfied; much to the amusement of F., who only laughs at what he is pleased to call my absurd interest in these poor creatures. But you know M——, I always *did* "take" to Indians; though it must be said, that those who bear that name here, have little resemblance to the glorious forest heroes that live in the Leather Stocking Tales; and in spite of my desire to find in them something poetical and interesting, a stern regard for truth, compels me to acknowledge, that the dusky beauty above described, is the only even moderately *pretty* squaw that I have ever seen.

At noon we stopped at the Buckeye Rancho for about an hour, and then pushed merrily on for the Pleasant Valley Rancho, which we expected to reach about sundown. Will you—*can* you believe that we got lost again? Should you travel over this road, you would not be at all surprised at the repetition of this misfortune. Two miles this side of Pleasant Valley,—which is very large,—there is a wide, bare plain of red stones, which one is compelled to cross in order to reach it, and I should not think that even in the day time any one but an Indian could keep the trail in this place. It was here, that just at dark, we probably missed the path, and entered about the centre of the Valley at the opposite side of an extensive grove from that on which the Rancho is situated. When I first began to suspect that we might possibly have to camp out another night, I *Caud-leized* at a great rate, but when it became a fixed fact, that such was our fate, I was instantly as mute and patient as the widow Prettyman when she succeeded to the throne of the venerated woman referred to above. Indeed, feeling perfectly well, and not being much fatigued, I should rather have enjoyed it, had not F——, poor fellow, been so grieved at the idea of my going supperless to a moss-stuffed couch. It was a long time before I could coax him to give up searching for the Rancho; and in truth, I should think that we rode round that part of the valley in which we found ourselves, for more than two hours, trying to find it.

About eleven o'clock we went back into the woods and camped for the night. Our bed was quite comfortable, and my saddle made an excellent pillow. Being so much higher in the mountains, we were a little chilly; and I was disturbed two or three times by a distant noise, which I have since been told was the growling of grizzly bears, that abounded in that vicinity. On the whole, we passed a comfortable night, and rose at sunrise, feeling perfectly refreshed and well. In less than an hour, we were eating breakfast at Pleasant Valley Ranch, which we easily discovered by daylight.

Here they informed us that "we had escaped a great marcy"—as old Jim used to say in relating his successful run from the wolf—inasmuch as the "grizzlies" had not devoured us during the night! But seriously, dear M——, my heart thrills with gratitude to the Father, for his tender care of us during that journey, which, view it as lightly as we may, was certainly attended with *some* danger.

Notwithstanding we had endured so much fatigue, I

felt as well, as ever I did, and after breakfast insisted upon
pursuing our journey, although F—— anxiously advised
me to defer it until next day. But imagine the horror, the
creme de la creme of borosity, of remaining for twelve
mortal hours of wakefulness, in a filthy, uncomfortable,
flea-haunted shanty, without books or papers, when Rich
Bar,—easily attainable before night, through the loveliest
scenery, shining in the yellow splendor of an autumnal
morning—lay before us! *I* had no idea of any such absurd
self-immolation. So we again started on our strange,
eventful journey.

I wish I could give you some faint idea of the majestic
solitudes through which we passed; where the pine trees
rise so grandly in their awful height, that they seem looking into Heaven itself. Hardly a living thing disturbed this
solemnly beautiful wilderness. Now and then a tiny lizard
glanced in and out among the mossy roots of the old trees,
or a golden butterfly flitted languidly from blossom to
blossom. Sometimes a saucy little squirrel would gleam
along the sombre trunk of some ancient oak, or a bevy of
quails, with their pretty, tufted heads and short, quick
tread, would trip athwart our path. Two or three times, in
the radiant distance, we descried a stately deer, which,
framed in by embowering leaves, and motionless as a
tableau, gazed at us for a moment with its large, limpid
eyes, then bounded away with the speed of light into the
evergreen depths of those glorious old woods.

Sometimes we were compelled to cross broad plains,
acres in extent, called *chaparrals*, covered with low shrubs
which, leafless and barkless, stand like vegetable skeletons
along the dreary waste. You cannot imagine what a weird
effect these eldritch bushes had upon my mind. Of a
ghastly whiteness, they at first reminded me of a planta-
tion of antlers, and I amused myself by fancying them a

herd of crouching deer; but they grew so wan and ghastly, that I began to look forward to the creeping across a *chaparral*,—(it is no easy task for the mules to wind through them,) with almost a feeling of dread.

But what a lovely sight greeted our enchanted eyes, as we stopped for a few moments on the summit of the hill leading into Rich Bar. Deep in the shadowy nooks of the far down valleys, like wasted jewels dropped from the radiant sky above, lay half a dozen blue-bosomed lagoons, glittering and gleaming and sparkling in the sunlight, as though each tiny wavelet were formed of rifted diamonds. It was worth the whole wearisome journey, danger from Indians, grizzly bears, sleeping under the stars, and all, to behold this beautiful vision. While I stood breathless with admiration, a singular sound and an exclamation of "A rattlesnake!" from F——, startled me into common sense again. I gave one look at the reptile, horribly beautiful, like a chain of living opals,—as it cork-screwed itself into that peculiar spiral, which it is compelled to assume in order to make an attack, and then fear overcoming curiosity—although I had never seen one of them before—I galloped out of its vicinity, as fast as my little mule could carry me.

The hill leading into Rich Bar is five miles long, and as steep as you can imagine. Fancy yourself riding for this distance, along the edge of a frightful precipice, where should your mule make a misstep, you would be dashed hundreds of feet into the awful ravine below. Every one we met tried to discourage us, and said that it would be impossible for me to ride down it. They would take F—— aside, much to my amusement, and tell him that he was assuming a great responsibility in allowing me to undertake such a journey. I however insisted upon going on. About half way down, we came to a level spot a few feet in

extent, covered with sharp slate-stones Here, the girth of
my saddle,—which we afterward found to be fastened
only by four *tacks* gave way, and I fell over the right side
striking on my left elbow. Strange to say, I was not in the
least hurt; and again my heart wept tearful thanks to God;
for had the accident happened at any other part of the
hill, I must have been dashed, a piece of shapeless nothing-
ness, into the dim valleys beneath.

F—— soon mended the saddle-girth, I mounted my
darling little mule, and rode triumphantly into Rich Bar,
at five o'clock in the evening. The Rich Bar-ians are astonished at my courage in daring to ride down the hill. Many
of the miners have told me that they dismounted several
times while descending it. I of course feel very vain of my
exploit, and glorify myself accordingly; being particularly
careful all the time not to inform my admirers, that my
courage was the result of the know nothing, fear nothing
principle; for I was certainly ignorant, until I had passed
them, of the dangers of the passage. Another thing that
prevented my dismounting, was the apparently utter im-
possibility, on such a steep and narrow path of mounting
again. Then I had much more confidence in my mule's
power of picking the way and keeping his footing than in
my own. It is the prettiest sight in the world to see these
cunning creatures, stepping so daintily and cautiously
among the rocks. Their pretty little feet, which absolutely
do not look larger than a silver dollar, seem made on purpose for the task. They are often perfect little vixens with
their masters, but an old mountaineer who has ridden
them for twenty years, told me that he never knew one to
be skittish with a woman. The intelligent darlings seem to
know what a bundle of helplessness they are carrying, and
scorn to take advantage of it.

We are boarding at present at the "Empire,"—a huge

shingle palace in the centre of Rich Bar,—which I will describe in my next letter. Pardon dear M—— the excessive egotism of this letter; but you have often flattered me by saying that my epistles were only interesting, when profusely illuminated, by that manuscriptal decoration represented by a great I. A most intense love of the ornament myself, makes it easy for me to believe you, and doubt not that my future communications will be as profusely stained with it as even you could desire.

LETTER SECOND

A TRIP INTO THE MINES

Rich Bar,
East Branch of the North Fork of Feather River,
September 15, 1851

DEAR M.—I believe that I closed my last letter by informing you that I was safely ensconced—afer all the hair-
breadth escapes of my wearisome, though at the same
time, delightful journey—under the magnificent roof of
the "Empire," which, by the way is *the* hotel of the place;
not but that nearly every other shanty on the Bar claims
the same grandiloquent title. Indeed, for that matter, California herself might be called the Hotel State, so completely is she inundated with taverns, boardinghouses, &c.
The Empire is the only two-story building in town, and
absolutely has a live "up-stairs." Here you will find two or
three glass windows, an unknown luxury in all the other
dwellings. It is built of planks of the roughest possible description; the roof, of course, is covered with canvas,
which also forms the entire front of the house, on which is
painted in immense capitals, the following imposing letters: "*THE EMPIRE!*" I will describe, as exactly as possible, this grand establishment. You first enter a large
apartment, level with the street, part of which is fitted up
as a bar-room, with that eternal crimson calico, which
flushes the whole social life of the "Golden State," with
its everlasting red—in the centre of a fluted mass of which,
gleams a really elegant mirror, set off by a back-ground of
decanters, cigar vases and jars of brandied fruit; the whole
forming a *tout ensemble* of dazzling splendor. A table
covered with a green cloth,—upon which lies a pack of

monte cards, a backgammon board, and a sickening pile of
"yellow kivered" literature,—with several uncomfortable
looking benches, complete the furniture of this most important portion of such a place as "The Empire." The remainder of the room does duty as a shop; where velveteen
and leather, flannel shirts and calico ditto—the latter
starched to an appalling state of stiffness—lie cheek by
jowl with hams, preserved meats, oysters and other groceries, in hopeless confusion. From the bar-room you as-
cend by four steps into the parlor, the floor of which is
covered by a straw carpet. This room contains quite a decent looking-glass, a sofa fourteen feet long, and a foot
and a half wide, painfully suggestive of an aching back—of
course covered with red calico, (the sofa, *not* the back,)—a
round table with a green cloth, six cane-bottom chairs, red
calico curtains, a cooking stove, a rocking chair, and a
woman and a baby, of whom more anon—the latter wearing a scarlet frock, to match the sofa and curtains. A flight
of four steps leads from the parlor to the upper story;
where, on each side of a narrow entry, are four eight feet
by ten bed-rooms, the floors of which are covered by
straw matting. Here your eyes are again refreshed with a
glittering vision of red calico curtains, gracefully festooned above wooden windows, picturesquely lattice-
like. These tiny chambers are furnished with little tables
covered with oil-cloth, and bedsteads so heavy that nothing short of a giant's strength could move them. Indeed, I
am convinced that they were built, piece by piece, on the
spot where they now stand. The entire building is lined
with purple calico, alternating with a delicate blue, and
the effect is really quite pretty. The floors are so very uneven, that you are always ascending a hill or descending
into a valley. The doors consist of a slight frame, covered
with dark blue drilling, and are hung on hinges of leather.
As to the kitchen and dining-room, I leave to your vivid

imagination to picture their primitiveness, merely observing, that nothing was ever more awkward and unwork-
manlike than the whole tenement. It is just such a piece of
carpentering as a child two years old, gifted with the
strength of a man, would produce, if it wanted to play at
making grown-up houses. And yet this impertinent apology for a house, costs its original owners more than eight
thousand dollars. This will not be quite so surprising,
when I inform you that at the time it was built, every
thing had to be packed from Marysville, at a cost of forty
cents a pound. Compare this with the price of freight on
the railroads at home, and you will easily make an esti-
mate of the immense outlay of money necessary to collect
the materials for such an undertaking at Rich Bar. It was
built by a company of gamblers, as a residence for two of
those unfortunates, who make a trade—a thing of barter—
of the holiest passion, when sanctified by *love*, that ever
thrills the wayward heart of poor humanity. To the lasting
honor of *miners* be it written, the *speculation* proved a
decided failure. Yes! these thousand men—many of whom
had been for years absent from the softening amenities of
female society, and the sweet restraining influences of
pure womanhood—these husbands of fair young wives,
kneeling daily at the altars of their holy homes, to pray for
their far-off ones—these sons of gray-haired mothers, majestic in their sanctified old age—these brothers of virginal
sisters, white and saint-like as the lilies of their own gar-
dens—looked only with contempt or pity upon these, oh,
so earnestly to be compassionated creatures! These unhappy members of a class, to one of which, the tenderest
words that Jesus ever spake, were uttered—left in a few
weeks, absolutely driven away by public opinion. The disappointed gamblers sold the house to its present proprietor for a few hundred dollars.

Mr. B——, the landlord of the Empire, was a western far-

mer, who with his wife crossed the plains about two years
ago. Immediately on his arrival, he settled at a mining station, where he remained until last spring, when he removed to Rich Bar. Mrs. B—— is a gentle and amiable looking woman, about twenty-five years of age. She is an example of the terrible wear and tear to the complexion in
crossing the plains, hers having become, through exposure
at that time, of a dark and permanent yellow, anything
but becoming. I will give you a key to her character which
will exhibit it better than weeks of description. She took a
nursing babe of eight months old, from her bosom, and
left it with two other children—almost infants—to cross
the plains in search of gold! When I arrived, she was cooking supper for some half-a-dozen people, while her really
pretty boy, who lay kicking furiously in his champagne
basket cradle, and screaming with a six months' old baby
power, had that day completed just two weeks of his
earthly pilgrimage. The inconvenience which she suffered
during what George Sand calls "the sublime martyrdom
of maternity," would appal the wife of the humblest
pauper of a New England village. Another woman, also
from the west, was with her at the time of her infant's
birth, but scarcely had the "latest found," gave the first
characteristic shriek of its debut upon the stage of life,
when this person was herself taken seriously ill, and was
obliged to return to her own cabin, leaving the poor exhausted mother entirely alone! Her husband lay dangerously sick himself at the time and of course could offer
her no assistance. A miner, who lived in the house, and
boarded himself, carried her some bread and tea in the
morning and evening, and that was all the care she had.
Two days after its birth she made a desperate effort, and
by easy stages of ten minutes at a time, contrived to get
poor baby washed and dressed after a fashion. He is an

astonishingly large and strong child, holds his head up like a six monther, and has but one failing, a too evident and officious desire to inform everybody, far and near, at all hours of the night and day, that his lungs are in a perfectly sound and healthy condition;—a piece of intelligence, which though very gratifying, is rather inconvenient if one happens to be particularly sleepy.

Beside Mrs. B——, there are three other women on the Bar. One is called "The Indiana Girl," from the name of her Pa's hotel; though it must be confessed that the sweet name of *girl* seems sadly incongruous, when applied to such a gigantic piece of humanity. I have a great desire to see her, which will probably not be gratified, as she leaves in a few days for the valley. But at any rate I can say that I have *heard* her. The far-off roll of her mighty voice, booming through two closed doors and a long entry, added greatly to the severe attack of nervous headache, under which I was suffering when she called. This gentle creature—wears the thickest kind of miners' boots, and has the dainty habit of wiping her dishes on her apron! Last spring she *walked* to this place, and packed fifty pounds of flour on her back down that awful hill—the snow being five feet deep at the time.

Mr. and Mrs. B——, who have three pretty children reside in a log cabin at the entrance of the village. One of the little girls was in the bar-room to-day, and her sweet and bird-like voice, brought tearfully and yet joyfully to my memory, "Tearsoul," "Leilie," and "Lile Katie."

Mrs. B.——, who is as small as the "Indiana Girl" is large, (indeed, I have been confidently informed that she weighs but sixty-eight pounds,) keeps, with her husband, the "Miners' Home;"—Mem—the lady tends bar. "*Voila*," my dear, the female population of my new home—splendid materials for social parties this winter, are they not.

LETTER THIRD

A TRIP INTO THE MINES

Rich Bar,
East Branch of the North Fork of Feather River,
September 20, 1851

I INTEND to-day, dear M., to be as disagreeably statistical
and as praiseworthily matter-of-factish as the most dogged utilitarian could desire. I shall give you a full, true and
particular account of the discovery, rise and progress of
this place, with a religious adherence to *dates* which will
rather astonish your unmathematical mind. But let me
first describe the spot, as it looked to my wondering and
unaccustomed eyes. Remember, I had never seen a mining
district before; and had just left San Francisco, amid
whose flashy-looking shops and showy houses the most of
my time had been spent, since my arrival into the Golden
State. Of course, to me, the *coup d'oeuil* of Rich Bar was
charmingly fresh and original. Imagine a tiny valley, about
eight hundred yards in length and, perhaps, thirty in
width, [it was measured for my especial information,] apparently hemmed in by lofty hills, almost perpendicular,
draperied to their very summits with beautiful fir trees;
the blue-bosomed "Plumas," or Feather River I suppose I
must call it, undulating along their base, and you have as
good an idea as I can give you of the *locale* of "Barra
Rica," as the Spaniards so prettily term it.

24

In almost any of the numerous books written upon California, no doubt you will be able to find a most scientific description of the origin of these "Bars." I must acknowledge, with shame, that my ideas on the subject are distressingly vague. I could never appreciate the poetry or the humor, of making one's wrists ache by knocking to pieces gloomy looking stones, or in dirtying one's fingers by analysing soils, in a vain attempt to fathom the osteology, or anatomy of our beloved earth; though my heart is thrillingly alive to the faintest shade of color and the infinite variety of styles in which she delights to robe her ever-changeful and ever-beautiful *surface*. In my unscientific mind the *formations* are without form and void; and you might as well talk Chinese to me, as to embroider your conversation with the terms "horn-blende," "mica," "lime-stone," "slate," "granite" and "quartz," in a hopeless attempt to enlighten me as to their merits. The dutiful diligence with which I attend course after course of lectures on Geology by America's greatest illustrator of that subject, arose rather from my affectionate reverence for our beloved Dr. H., and the fascinating charm which his glorious mind throws round every subject which it condescends to illuminate, than to any interest in the dry science itself. It is, therefore, with a most humiliating consciousness of my geological deficiencies, that I offer you the only explanation which I have been able to obtain from those most learned in such matters here. I gather from their remarks, that these bars are formed by deposits of earth, rolling down from the mountains, crowding the river aside and occupying a portion of its deserted bed. If my definition is unsatisfactory, I can but refer you to some of the aforesaid works upon California.

Through the middle of Rich Bar runs the street, thickly planted with about forty tenements; among which figure round tents, square tents, plank hovels, log cabins, &c.,—the residences, varying in elegance and convenience from the palatial splendor of "The Empire," down to a "local habitation," formed of pine boughs, and covered with old calico shirts.

To-day I visited the "Office;" the only one on the river. I had heard so much about it from others, as well as from F., that I really *did* expect something extra. When I entered this imposing place, the shock to my optic nerves was so great that I sank, helplessly, upon one of the benches which ran, divan-like, the whole length (ten feet!) of the building, and laughed till I cried. There was, of course, no floor; a rude nondescript in one corner, on which was ranged the medical library, consisting of half a dozen volumes, did duty as a table. The shelves, which looked like sticks snatched hastily from the wood-pile and nailed up without the least alteration, contained quite a respectable array of medicines. The white canvas window stared everybody in the face, with the interesting information painted on it, in perfect grenadiers of capitals, that this was Dr.———'s office.

At my loud laugh, (which, it must be confessed, was noisy enough to give the whole street assurance of the presence of a woman,) F. looked shocked, and his partner looked prussic acid. To him, (the partner, I mean, he hadn't been out of the mines for years)—the "Office" was a thing sacred and set apart for an almost admiring worship. It was a beautiful, architectural ideal, embodied in pine shingles and cotton cloth. Here, he literally "lived, and moved, and had his being," his bed and his board. With an admiration of the fine arts, truly praiseworthy, he had fondly decorated the walls thereof with sundry pictures from Godey, Graham and Sartain's Magazines, among which, fashion plates with imaginary monsters,

sporting miraculous waists, impossible wrists and fabulous feet, largely predominated.

During my call at the office, I was introduced to one of
the *finders* of Rich Bar—a young Georgian, who afterwards gave me a full description of all the facts connected
with its discovery. This unfortunate had not spoken to a
woman for two years; and in the elation of his heart at the
joyful event, he rushed out and invested capital in some
excellent champagne, which I, on Willie's principle of
"doing in Turkey as the Turkies do," assisted the company in drinking to the honor of my own arrival. I mention this, as an instance, that nothing can be done in California without the sanctifying influence of the *spirit*; and
it generally appears in much more "questionable shape"
than that of sparkling wine. Mr. H. informed me, that on
the twentieth of July, 1850, it was rumored at Nelson's
Creek—a mining station situated at the Middle Fork of the
Feather River, about eighty miles from Marysville—that
one of those vague "Somebodies"—a near relation of the
"They Says"—had discovered mines of a remarkable richness in a north-easterly direction, and about forty miles
from the first-mentioned place. Anxious and immediate
search was made for "Somebody," but, as our western
brethren say, he "wasn't thar!" But his absence could not
deter the miners when once the golden rumor had been set
afloat. A large company packed up their goods and chat-
tels, generally consisting of a pair of blankets, a frying-
pan, some flour, salt pork, brandy, pick-axe and shovel,
and started for the new Dorado. They "traveled, and traveled, and traveled," as we used to say in the fairy stories,
for nearly a week in every possible direction, when one
evening, weary and discouraged, about one hundred of
the party found themselves at the top of that famous hill,
which figures so largely in my letters, whence the river can

be distinctly seen. Half of the number concluded to descend the mountain that night, the remainder stopping on
the summit until the next morning. On arriving at Rich
Bar, part of the adventurers camped there, but many went
a few miles further down the river. The next morning two
men turned over a large stone, beneath which they found
quite a sizable piece of gold. They washed a small panful
of the dirt, and obtained from it two hundred and fifty-six
dollars. Encouraged by this success, they commenced
staking off the legal amount of ground allowed to each
person for mining purposes; and, the remainder of the
party having descended the hill, before night the entire
bar was "claimed." In a fortnight from that time, the two
men who found the first bit of gold had each taken out six
thousand dollars. Two others took out thirty-three
pounds of gold in eight hours; which is the best day's work
that has been done on this branch of the river; the largest
amount ever taken from one panful of dirt was fifteen
hundred dollars. In little more than a week after its discovery, five hundred men had settled upon the bar for the
summer.—Such is the wonderful alacrity with which a
mining town is built. Soon after was discovered on the
same side of the river—about half a mile apart, and at
nearly the same distance from this place—the two bars,
"Smith" and "Indian," both very rich; also another, lying
across the river, just opposite Indian, called "Missouri
Bar." There are several more, all within a few miles of
here, called "Frenchman's," "Taylor's," "Brown's,"
"The Junction," "Wyandott" and "Muggin's." But they
are at present of little importance as mining stations.

Those who worked in these mines during the fall of
1850 were extremely fortunate; but, alas! the Monte
fiend ruined hundreds! Shall I tell you the fate of two of
the most successful of these gold hunters? From poor

men, they found themselves at the end of a few weeks, absolutely rich. Elated with their good fortune, seized with a mania for Monte, in less than a year, these unfortunates,—so lately respectable and intelligent,—became a pair of drunken gamblers. One of them at this present writing, works for five dollars a day and boards himself out of that; the other actually suffers for the necessaries of life,—a too common result of scenes in the mines.

There were but a few that dared to remain in the mountains during the winter for fear of being buried in the snow; of which at that time they had a most vague idea. I have been told that in these sheltered valleys it seldom falls to the depth of more than a foot, and disappears almost invariably within a day or two. Perhaps there were three hundred that concluded to stay; of which number, two-thirds stopped on Smith's Bar, as the labor of mining there is much easier than it is here. Contrary to the general expectation, the weather was delightful until about the middle of March; it then commenced storming, and continued to snow and rain incessantly for nearly three weeks. Supposing that the rainy season had passed, hundreds had arrived on the river during the previous month. The snow, which fell several feet in depth on the mountains, rendered the trail impassable and entirely stopped the pack trains; provisions soon became scarce, and the sufferings of these unhappy men were, indeed, extreme. Some adventurous spirits, with true Yankee hardihood, forced their way through the snow to the Frenchman's ranch, and packed flour *on their backs*, for more than forty miles! The first meal that arrived sold for three dollars a pound. Many subsisted for days on nothing but barley, which is kept here to feed the pack-mules on. One unhappy individual who could not obtain even a little barley, for love or money, and had eaten nothing for three days, forced his way out to the Spanish rancho fourteen miles distant, and in less than an hour after his arrival, had devoured *twenty-seven* biscuit and a corresponding quantity of other eatables, and, of course, drinkables to match. Don't let this account alarm you. There is no danger of another famine here. They tell me that there is hardly a building in the place that has not food enough in it to last its occupants for the next two years; besides, there are two or three well-filled groceries in town.

LETTER FOURTH

A TRIP INTO THE MINES

Rich Bar,
East Branch of the North Fork of Feather River,
September 22, 1851

THERE HAS been quite an excitement here for the last week, on account of a successful amputation having been performed upon the person of a young man by the name of W. As I happen to know all the circumstances of the case, I will relate them to you, as illustrative of the frightful accidents to which the gold-seekers are constantly liable; and I can assure you that similar ones happen very often. W. was one of the first who settled on this river, and suffered extremely from the scarcity of provisions during the last winter. By steady industry in his laborious vocation, he had accumulated about four thousand dollars. He was thinking seriously of returning to Massachusetts with what he had already gained, when in the early part of last May, a stone unexpectedly rolling from the top of Smith's Hill, on the side of which he was mining—crushed his leg in the most shocking manner. Naturally enough, the poor fellow shrank with horror, from the idea of an amputation here in the mountains; it seemed absolutely worse than death. His physician, appreciating his feelings on the subject, made every effort to save his shattered limb; but, truly, the fates seemed against him. An attack of typhoid fever reduced him to a state of great weakness, which was still further increased by erysipelas—a common complaint in the mountains—in its most virulent form; the latter disease settling in the fractured leg, rendered a cure utterly hopeless. His sufferings have been of the most intense de-

scription. Through all the blossoming spring, and a summer as golden as its own golden self, of our beautiful California, he has languished away existence in a miserable
cabin, his only nurses men—some of them, it is true, kind
and good—others neglectful and careless. A few weeks
since, F. was called in to see him. He decided immediately
that nothing but an amputation would save him. A universal outcry against it, was raised by nearly all the other
physicians on the Bar. They agreed *en masse*, that he
could live but a few weeks, unless the leg—now a mere
lump of disease—was taken off; at the same time, they declared that he would certainly expire under the knife, and
that it was cruel to subject him to any further suffering.
You can, perhaps, imagine F.'s anxiety. It was a great responsibility for a young physician to take. Should the
patient die during the operation, F.'s professional reputa-
tion would, of course, die with him. But he felt it his duty
to waive all selfish considerations, and give W. that one
chance—feeble as it seemed—for his life. Thank God, the
result was most triumphant! For several days, existence
hung upon a mere thread. He was not allowed to speak or
move, and was fed from a teaspoon—his only diet being
milk, which we obtained from the Spanish Rancho, send-
ing twice a week for it. I should have mentioned that F.
decidedly refused to risk an operation in the small and
miserable tent in which W. had languished away nearly
half a year, and he was removed to the "Empire," the day
previous to the amputation. It is almost needless to tell
you that the little fortune, to accumulate which he suffered so much—is now nearly exhausted. Poor fellow! the
philosophy and cheerful resignation, with which he has
endured his terrible martyrdom, is beautiful to behold.
My heart aches as I look upon his young face, and think of
"his gentle, dark-eyed mother, weeping lonely at the
North," for her far away and suffering son.

As I sat by the bedside of our poor invalid, yielding myself up to a world of dreamy visionings, suggested by the musical sweep of the pine branch which I waved above his head, and the rosy sunset flushing the western casement with its soft glory, he suddenly opened his languid eyes and whispered, "the Chileno procession is returning; do you not hear it?" I did not tell him

> "That the weary sound, and the heavy breath,
> And the silent motions of passing death,
> And the smell, cold, oppressive and dank,
> Sent through the pores of the coffin plank,"

had already informed me that a far other band than that of the noisy South Americans, was solemnly marching by. It was the funeral train of a young man who was instantly killed, the evening before, by falling into one of those deep pits, sunk for mining purposes, which are scattered over the bar in almost every direction. I rose quietly and looked from the window. About a dozen persons were carrying an unpainted coffin, without pall or bier (the place of the latter being supplied by ropes) up the steep hill which rises behind the Empire—on the top of which, is situated the burial ground of Rich Bar. The bearers were all neatly and cleanly dressed in their miner's costume; which, consisting of a flannel shirt,—almost always of a dark blue color—pantaloons with the boots drawn up over them, and a low-crowned, broad-brimmed, black felt hat—though the fashion of the latter is not invariable—is not, simple as it seems, so unpicturesque as you might, perhaps, imagine. A strange horror of that lonely mountain grave-yard came over me, as I watched the little company wending wearily up to the solitary spot. The "sweet habitude of being,"—not that I fear *death*, but that I love *life*, as, for instance, Charles Lamb loved it,—makes me

particularly affect a cheerful burial-place. I know that it is
dreadfully unsentimental, but I should like to make my
last home in the heart of a crowded city; or better still, in
one of those social homes of the dead, which the Turks,
with a philosophy so beautiful and so poetical, make their
most cheerful resort. Singularly enough, Christians seem
to delight in rendering death particularly hideous, and
grave-yards decidedly disagreeable. I, on the contrary,
would "plant the latter with laurels, and sprinkle it with
lilies." I would wreath "Sleep's pale brother" so thickly
with roses, that even those rabid moralists, who think that
it makes us better, to paint him as a dreadful fiend, instead
of a loving friend—could see nothing but their blushing
radiance. I would alter the whole paraphernalia of the
coffin, the shroud and the bier; particularly the first,
which, as Dickens says, "looks like a high-shouldered
ghost, with its hands in its breeches pockets." Why should
we endeavor to make our entrance into a glorious immortality, so unutterably ghastly? Let us glide into the "fair
shadow land" through a "gate of flowers," if we may no
longer, as in the majestic olden time, aspire heavenward
on the wings of perfumed flame.

How oddly do life and death jostle each other in this
strange world of ours! How nearly allied are smiles and
tears! My eyes were yet moist from the egotistical *pitie de
moimeme* in which I had been indulging, at the thought of
sleeping forever amid these lonely hills, which in a few
years must return to their primeval solitude, perchance
never again to be awakened by the voice of humanity—
when the Chileno procession, every member of it most intensely drunk, really *did* appear. I never saw anything
more diverting than the whole affair. Of course, *selon
regle*, I ought to have been shocked and horrified—to have
shed salt tears, and have uttered melancholy Jeremiads

over their miserable degradation. But the world is so full
of platitudes, my dear, that I think you will easily forgive
me for not boring you with a temperance lecture, and will
good-naturedly let me have my laugh, and not think me
very wicked after all.

You must know that to-day is the anniversary of the
Independence of Chile. The procession got up in honor of
it, consisted, perhaps, of twenty men, nearly a third of
whom, were of that class of Yankees, who are particularly
noisy and particularly conspicuous in all celebrations,
where it is each man's most onerous duty, to get, what is
technically called "tight." The man who headed the procession was a complete comic poem in his own individual
self. He was a person of Falstaffean proportions and color-
ing; and if a brandy barrel ever *does* "come alive," and,
donning a red shirt and buck-skin trowsers, betake itself
to pedestrianism, it will look more like my hero than anything else that I can at present think of. With that affec-
tionateness so peculiar to people when they arrive at the
sentimental stage of intoxication—although it was with
the greatest difficulty that he could sustain his own cor-
porocity—he was tenderly trying to direct the zigzag
footsteps of his companion, a little withered-up, weird-
looking Chileno. Alas, for the wickedness of human
nature! The latter, whose drunkenness had taken a Byron-
ic and misanthropical turn, rejected with the basest ingra-
titude, these delicate attentions. Do not think that my in-
carnated brandy cask was the only one of the party "who
did unto others as he would they should do unto him;" for
the entire band were officiously tendering to each other
the same good Samaritan-like assistance. I was not astonished at the Virginia fence-like style of their marching,
when I heard a description of the feast of which they had
partaken a few hours before. A friend of mine who

stopped into the tent where they were dining, said that the board—really *board*—was arranged with a bottle of claret at each plate; and after the cloth—metaphorically speaking, I mean, for table-linen is a mere myth in the mines—was removed, a twenty-gallon keg of brandy was placed in the centre, with quart-dippers gracefully encircling it, that each one might help himself as he pleased. Can you wonder, after that, that every man vied with his neighbor in illustrating Hogarth's line of beauty? It was impossible to tell which nation was the most gloriously drunk; but this I *will* say, even at the risk of being thought partial to my own beloved countrymen; "that though the Chilenos reeled with a better grace, the Americans did it more *naturally!*

LETTER FIFTH

A TRIP INTO THE MINES

Rich Bar,
East Branch of the North Fork of Feather River,
September 22, 1851

IT SEEMS indeed awful, dear M., to be compelled to announce to you the death of one of the four women forming the female population of this Bar. I have just returned from the funeral of poor Mrs. B., who died of peritonitis, (a common disease in this place) after an illness of four days only. Our hostess herself heard of her sickness but two days since. On her return from a visit which she had paid to the invalid, she told me that although Mrs. B.'s family did not seem alarmed about her, in her opinion she would not survive but a few hours. Last night we were startled by the frightful news of her decease. Confess, that without being egotistical, the death of one out of a community of four women, might well alarm the remainder.

Her funeral took place at ten this morning. The family reside in a log-cabin at the head of the Bar; and, although it had no window—all the light admitted, entering through an aperture where there *will* be a door when it becomes cold enough for such a luxury—yet I am told, and can easily believe that it is one of the most *comfortable* residences in the place. I observed it particularly, for it was the first log-cabin that I had ever seen. Everything in the room, though of the humblest description, was exceedingly clean and neat.

On a board, supported by two butter-tubs, was extended the body of the dead woman, covered with a sheet; by its side stood the coffin of unstained pine, lined with white cambric. You, who have alternately laughed and scolded at my provoking and inconvenient deficiency in the power of observing, will, perhaps, wonder at the minuteness of my descriptions; but I know how deeply you are interested in everything relating to California, and therefore I take pains to describe things exactly as I *see* them, hoping that thus you will obtain an idea of life in the mines, *as it is.*

The bereaved husband held in his arms a sickly babe ten months old, which was moaning piteously for its mother. The other child, a handsome, bold-looking little girl six years of age, was running gaily around the room, perfectly unconscious of her great bereavement. A sickening horror came over me, to see her every few moments, run up to her dead mother, and peep laughingly under the handkerchief, that covered her moveless face. Poor little thing! It was evident that her baby-toilet had been made by men; she had on a new calico dress, which, having no tucks in it, trailed to the floor, and gave her a most singular and dwarf-womanly appearance.

About twenty men, with the three women of the place, had assembled at the funeral. An *extempore* prayer was made, filled with all the peculiarities usual to that style of petition. Ah! how different from the soothing verses of the glorious burial service of the church.

As the procession started for the hill-side grave-yard—a dark cloth cover, borrowed from a neighboring monte-table, was flung over the coffin. Do not think that I mention any of these circumstances in a spirit of mockery; far from it. Every observance, usual on such occasions, that was *procurable*, surrounded this funeral. All the gold on Rich Bar could do no more; and should I die to-morrow, I should be marshaled to my mountain grave beneath the same monte-table cover pall, which shrouded the coffin of poor Mrs. B.

I almost forgot to tell you, how painfully the feelings of
the assembly were shocked by the sound of the nails—
there being no screws at any of the shops—driven with a
hammer into the coffin, while closing it. It seemed as if it
must disturb the pale sleeper within.

To-day I called at the residence of Mrs. R. It is a canvas
house, containing a suite of three "apartments,"—as Dick
Swiveller would say—which, considering that they were
all on the ground floor, are kept surprisingly neat. There is
a bar-room, blushing all over with red calico, a dining-
room, kitchen and a small bed-closet. The little sixty-
eight-pounder woman is queen of the establishment. By
the way, a man who walked home with us, was enthusiastic in her praise. "Magnificent woman that, sir," he said,
addressing my husband; "a wife of the right sort, *she* is.
Why," he added, absolutely rising into eloquence as he
spoke, "she earnt her *old man*," (said individual twenty-
one years of age, perhaps,) "nine hundred dollars in nine
weeks, clear of all expenses, by washing! Such women
ain't common, I tell *you*; if they were, a man might marry,
and make money by the operation." I looked at this person with somewhat the same kind of *inverted* admiration,
wherewith Leigh Hunt was wont to gaze upon that friend
of his, "who used to elevate the common-place to a pitch
of the sublime;" and he looked at *me* as if to say, that,
though by no means gloriously arrayed, I was a mere cum-
berer of the ground; inasmuch as I toiled not, neither did I
wash. Alas! I hung my diminished head; particularly when
I remembered the eight dollars a dozen, which I had been
in the habit of paying for the washing of linen-cambric
pocket-handkerchiefs while in San Francisco. But a lucky
thought came into my mind. As all men cannot be Napoleon Bonapartes, so all women cannot be *manglers*; the
majority of the sex must be satisfied with simply being
mangled. Re-assured by this idea, I determined to meekly

and humbly pay the amount per dozen required to enable this really worthy and agreeable little woman "to lay up her hundred dollars a week, clear of expenses." But is it not wonderful, what femininity is capable of? To look at the tiny hands of Mrs. R., you would not think it possible, that they could wring out anything larger than a doll's night-cap. But, as is often said, nothing is strange in California. I have known of sacrifices, requiring, it would seem, superhuman efforts, made by women in this country, who at home were nurtured in the extreme of elegance and delicacy.

Mr. B. called on us to-day with little Mary. I tried to make her, at least, look sad, as I talked about her mother; but although she had seen the grave closed over her coffin —for a friend of her father's had carried her in his arms to the burial—she seemed laughingly indifferent to her loss. Being myself an orphan, my heart contracted painfully at her careless gaiety, when speaking of her dead parent, and I said to our hostess, "what a cold-blooded little wretch it is!" But immediately my conscience struck me with remorse. Poor orphaned one! Poor bereaved darling! Why should I so cruelly wish to darken her young life with that knowledge, which a few years experience will so painfully teach her? "All *my* mother came into my eyes," as I bent down and kissed the white lids, which shrouded her beautiful dark orbs; and, taking her fat little hand in mine, I led her to my room, where, in the penitence of my heart, I gave her everything that she desired. The little chatterer was enchanted, not having had any new playthings for a long while. It was beautiful to hear her pretty exclamations of ecstasy, at the sight of some tiny scent bottles, about an inch in length, which she called baby decanters.

Mr. B. intends, in a day or two, to take his children to their grandmother, who resides somewhere near Marys-

ville, I believe. This is an awful place for children; and nervous mothers would "die daily," if they could see little
Mary running fearlessly to the very edge of, and looking
down into these holes—many of them sixty feet in depth—
which have been excavated in the hope of finding gold,
and of course left open.

LETTER SIXTH

A TRIP INTO THE MINES

Rich Bar,
East Branch of the North Fork of Feather River,
September 30, 1851

I THINK that I have never spoken to you of the mournful extent to which profanity prevails in California. You know that at home it is considered *vulgar* for a gentleman to swear; but I am told that here, it is absolutely the fashion, and that people who never uttered an oath in their lives while in the "States," now "clothe themselves with curses as with a garment." Some try to excuse themselves by saying that it is a careless habit, into which they have glided imperceptibly, from having been compelled to associate so long with the vulgar and the profane; that it is a mere slip of the tongue, which means absolutely nothing, etc. I am willing to believe this, and to think as charitably as possible of many persons here, who have unconsciously adopted a custom which I know they abhor. Whether there is more profanity in the mines than elsewhere, I know not; but during the short time that I have been at Rich Bar, I have *heard* more of it than in all my life before. Of course, the most vulgar blackguard will abstain from swearing in the *presence* of a lady; but in this rag and card-board house, one is *compelled* to hear the most sacred of names constantly profaned by the drinkers and

gamblers who haunt the bar-room at all hours. And this is
a custom which the gentlemanly and quiet proprietor,
much as he evidently dislikes it, cannot possibly prevent.

Some of these expressions, were they not so fearfully
blasphemous, would be grotesquely sublime. For instance; not five minutes ago, I heard two men quarrelling
in the street, and one said to the other, "only let me get
hold of your beggarly carcase once, and I will use you up
so small that God Almighty himself cannot see your
ghost!"

To live thus in constant danger of being hushed to one's
rosy rest by a ghastly lullaby of oaths, is revolting in the
extreme. For that reason, and because it is infinitely more
comfortable during the winter season, than a plank-house,
F. has concluded to build a log-cabin, where, at least, I
shall not be *obliged* to hear the solemn names of the
Father and the dear Master so mockingly profaned.

But it is not the swearing alone which disturbs my slumber. There is a dreadful flume, the machinery of which,
keeps up the most dismal moaning and shrieking all the
livelong night—painfully suggestive of a suffering child.
But, oh dear! you don't know what that is, do you? Now,
if I was scientific, I would give you such a vivid description
of it, that you would see a pen and ink flume staring at
you from this very letter. But alas! my own ideas on the
subject, are in a state of melancholy vagueness. I will do
my possible, however, in the way of explanation. A flume,
then, is an immense trough, which takes up a portion of
the river, and, with the aid of a dam, compels it to run in
another channel, leaving the vacated bed of the stream
ready for mining purposes.

There is a gigantic project now on the *tapis* of fluming
the entire river for many miles, commencing a little above
Rich Bar. Sometimes these fluming companies are emi-

nently successful; at others, their operations are a dead failure.

But in truth, the whole mining system in California is one great gambling, or better perhaps—lottery transaction. It is impossible to tell whether a "claim" will prove valuable or not. F. has invariably sunk money on every one that he has bought. Of course, a man who works a "claim" himself, is more likely—even should it turn out poor—"to get his money back," as they say—than one who, like F., hires it done.

A few weeks since, F. paid a thousand dollars for a "claim," which has proved utterly worthless. He might better have thrown his money into the river than to have bought it; and yet some of the most experienced miners on the Bar, thought that it would "pay."

But I began to tell you about the different noises which disturb my peace of mind by day, and my repose of body by night, and have gone instead, into a financial disquisition upon mining prospects. Pray forgive me, even though I confess that I intend some day, when I feel *statistically* inclined, to bore you with some profound remarks upon the claiming, drifting, sluicing, ditching, fluming and coyoting politics of the "diggins."

But to return to my sleep murderers. The rolling on the bowling alley never leaves off for ten consecutive minutes at any time during the entire twenty-four hours. It is a favorite amusement at the mines; and the only difference that Sunday makes, is, that then it never leaves off for *one* minute.

Besides the flume and the bowling alley, there is an inconsiderate dog, which *will* bark from starry eve till dewy morn. I fancy that he has a wager on the subject, as all the other *puppies* seem bitten by the betting mania.

A propos of dogs; I found dear old Dake—the noble

New Foundland which H. gave us—looking as intensely black, and as grandly aristocratical as ever. He is the only high-bred dog on the river. There is another animal, by the plebeian name of John, (what a name for a *dog*!) really a handsome creature, which looks as if he might have a faint sprinkling of good blood in his veins. Indeed, I have thought it possible that his great-grandfather was a bull-dog. But he always barks at *me*—which I consider as proof positive that he is nothing but a low-born mongrel. To be sure, his master says, to excuse him, that he never saw a woman before; but a dog of any chivalry would have rec-ognized the gentler sex, even if it *was* the first time that he had been blessed with the sight.

In the first part of my letter, I alluded to the swearing propensities of the Rich Barians. Those of course would shock you; but though you hate slang, I know that you could not help smiling at some of their *bizarre* cant phrases.

For instance, if you tell a Rich Barian anything which he doubts, instead of simply asking you if it is true, he will *invariably* cock his head interrogatively, and almost pa-thetically address you with the solemn adjuration, "Hon-est Indian?" Whether this phrase is a slur or a compliment to the aboriginees of this country, I do not know.

Again; they will agree to a proposal, with the appropri-ate words, "Talk enough when horses fight!" which sen-tence they will sometimes slightly vary to "Talk enough between gentlemen."

If they wish to borrow anything of you, they will mildly inquire if you have it "about your clothes." As an illustration; a man asked F. the other day, "If he had a spare pick-axe about his clothes." And F. himself gravely inquired of me this evening at the dinner-table, if I had "a *pickle* about my clothes."

If they ask a man an embarrassing question, or in any way have placed him in an equivocal position, they will triumphantly declare that they have "got the dead-wood on him." And they are everlastingly "going narry cent" on those of whose credit they are doubtful. There are many others which may be common enough every where, but as I never happened to hear them before, they have for me all the freshness of originality. You know that it has always been one of my pet rages, to trace cant phrases to their origin; but most of those in vogue here, would, I verily believe, puzzle Horne Tooke himself.

LETTER SEVENTH

A TRIP INTO THE MINES

From our Log Cabin, Indian Bar,
October 7, 1851

YOU WILL perchance be surprised, dear M., to receive a letter from me dated Indian, instead of Rich Bar; but as many of F's most intimate friends reside at this settlement, he concluded to build his log cabin here.

Solemn council was held upon the ways and means of getting "Dame Shirley" to her new home. The general opinion was, that she had better mount her fat mule and ride over the hill, as all agreed that it was very doubtful whether she would be able to cross the logs and jump the rocks, which would bar her way by the water-passage. But that obstinate little personage, who has always been haunted with a passionate desire to do every thing which people said she could *not* do, made up her wilful mind immediately to go by the river. Behold then, the "Dame" on her winding way, escorted by a deputation of Indian Barian's, which had come up for that important purpose.

It is impossible, my sister, for any power of language over which *I* have command, to convey to you an idea of the wild grandeur and the awful magnificence of the scenery in this vicinity. This Fork of the Feather river, comes down very much "as the water does at Lodore;" now gliding along with a liquid measure, like a river in a dream, and anon bursting into a thousand glittering foam-beads over the huge rocks, which rise dark, solemn and weird-like, in its midst. The crossings are formed of logs, often moss-grown. Only think how charmingly picturesque, to eyes

47

wearied with the costly masonry, or carpentry of the
bridges at home. At every step gold diggers or their operations greet your vision. Sometimes in the form of a dam;
sometimes in that of a river, turned slightly from its channel, to aid the indefatigable gold hunters in their mining
projects. Now, on the side of a hill you will see a long-
tom,—a huge machine invented to facilitate the separation
of the ore from its native element; or a man busily engaged
in working a rocker,—a much smaller and simpler machine, used for the same object; or more primitive still,
some solitary prospecter, with a pan of dirt in his hands,
which he is carefully washing at the water's edge, to see if
he can "get the color," as it is technically phrased, which
means literally the smallest particle of gold.

As we approached Indian Bar, the path led several times
fearfully near deep holes, from which the laborers were
gathering their yellow harvest; and "Dame Shirley's"
small head swam dizzily as she crept shudderingly by.

The first thing which attracted my attention, as my
new home came in view, was the blended blue, red and
white of the American banner, undulating like a many-
colored snake amid the lofty verdure of the cedars which
garland the brown brow of the hill behind our cabin. This
flag was suspended on the Fourth of July last, by a patrio-
tic sailor, who climbed to the top of the tree to which he
attached it, cutting away the branches as he descended,
until it stood among its stately brethren, a beautiful moss-
wreathed Liberty pole, flinging to the face of Heaven the
glad colors of the Free.

When I attempt, dear M., to describe one of these spots
to you, I regret more than ever, the ill-health of my childhood, which prevented my obtaining any degree of excel-
lence in sketching from Nature. Had it not been for that
interruption to my artistic education, I might, with a few

touches of the pencil or the brush, give you the place and
its surroundings. But alas! my feeble pen will convey to
you a very faint idea of its savage beauty.

This bar is so small, that it seems impossible that the
tents and cabins scattered over it can amount to a dozen;
there are, however, twenty in all, including those formed
of calico shirts and pine boughs. With the exception of the
paths leading to the different tenements, the entire level is
covered with mining holes, on the edges of which lie the
immense piles of dirt and stones which have been removed
from the excavations. There is a deep pit in front of our
cabin and another at the side of it; though they are not
worked, as when "prospected," they did not "yield the
color."

Not a spot of verdure is to be seen on this place; but the
glorious hills rising on every side vested in foliage of living
green, make ample amends for the sterility of the tiny
level upon which we camp. The surrounding scenery is infinitely more charming than that of Rich Bar. The river in
hue of a vivid emerald—as if it reflected the hue of the fir
trees above,—bordered with a band of dark red, caused by
the streams flowing into it from the different sluices,
ditches, long-toms, etc., which meander from the hill just
back of the Bar, wanders musically along. Across the river
and in front of us, rises nearly perpendicularly, a group of
mountains, the summits of which are broken into many
beautifully cut conical and pyramidal peaks. At the foot
and left of these eminences, and a little below our Bar, lies
Missouri Bar, which is reached from this spot by a log
bridge. Around the latter, the river curves in the shape of a
crescent and singularly enough, the mountain rising behind this bend in the stream, outlines itself against the
lustrous Heaven, in a shape as exact and perfect as the
moon herself in her first quarter. Within one horn of this

crescent, the water is a mass of foam sparkles, and it plays upon the rocks which line its bed an everlasting dirge suggestive of the "grand forever" of the ocean.

At present the sun does not condescend to shine upon Indian Bar at all, and the old settlers tell me that he will not smile upon us for the next three months; but he nestles lovingly in patches of golden glory, all along the brows of the different hills around us, and now and then stoops to kiss the topmost wave on the opposite shore of the Rio de las Plumas.

The first artificial elegance which attracts your vision, is a large rag shanty, roofed, however, with a rude kind of shingles, over the entrance of which is painted in red capitals, ("to what base uses do we come at last,") the name of the great Humboldt spelt without the *d*. This is the only hotel in this vicinity, and as there is a really excellent bowling alley attached to it, and the bar-room has a floor upon which the miners can dance, and, above all, a cook who can play the violin, it is very popular. But the clinking of glasses, and the swaggering air of some of the drinkers, reminds us that it is no place for a lady, so we will pass through the dining room and emerging at the kitchen, in a step or two reach our log cabin. Enter my dear; you are perfectly welcome; besides, we could not keep you out if we would, as there is not even a latch on the canvas door, though we really intend in a day or two to have a hook put on to it.

The room into which we have just entered is about twenty feet square. It is lined over the top with white cotton cloth, the breadths of which being sewed together only in spots, stretch apart in many places, giving one a birds-eye view of the shingles above. The sides are hung with a gaudy chintz, which I consider a perfect marvel of calico printing. The artist seems to have exhausted himself

on *roses;* from the largest cabbage, down to the tiniest
Burgundy, he has arranged them in every possible variety
of wreath, garland, bouquet, and single flower; they are of
all stages of growth, from earliest budhood up to the rav-
ishing beauty of the "last rose of summer." Nor has he
confined himself to the colors usually worn by this lovely
plant; but, with the daring of a great genius soaring above
nature, worshiping the ideal rather than the real, he has
painted them brown, purple, green, black and blue. It
would need a floral catalogue to give you the names of *all*
the varieties which bloom upon the calico; but, judging by
the shapes— which really are much like the originals—I can
swear to moss roses, Burgundies, York and Lancaster, tea
roses, and multi-floras.

A curtain of the above described chintz, (I shall hem it
at the first opportunity), divides off a portion of the
room, behind which stands a bedstead that in ponderosity
leaves the Empire couches far behind. But before I attempt the furniture let me finish describing the cabin
itself.

The fireplace is built of stones and mud, the chimney
finished off with alternate layers of rough sticks and this
same rude mortar; contrary to the usual custom, it is built
inside, as it was thought that arrangement would make the
room more comfortable; and you may imagine the queer
appearance of this unfinished pile of stones, mud and
sticks. The mantle-piece—remember that on this portion
of a great building, some artists, by their exquisite workmanship, have become world renowned—is formed of a
beam of wood, covered with strips of tin procured from
cans, upon which still remain in black hieroglyphics, the
names of the different eatables which they formerly contained. Two smooth stones—how delightfully primitive—
do duty as fire-dogs. I suppose that it would be no more

than civil to call a hole two feet square in one side of the room, a window, although it is as yet guiltless of glass. F. tried to coax the proprietor of the Empire to let him have a window from that pine and canvas palace; but he of course declined, as to part with it would really inconvenience himself; so F. has sent to Marysville for some glass, though it is the general opinion that the snow will render the trail impassable for mules before we can get it. In this case, we shall tack up a piece of cotton cloth, and should it chance at any time to be very cold, hang a blanket before the opening. At present the weather is so mild that it is pleasanter as it is, though we have a fire in the mornings and evenings, more, however, for luxury than because we really need it. For my part, I almost hope that we shall not be able to get any glass, for you will perhaps remember that it was a pet habit of mine, in my own room, to sit by a great fire in the depth of winter, with my window open.

One of our friends had nailed up an immense quantity of unhemmed cotton cloth—very coarse—in front of this opening, and as he evidently prided himself upon the elegant style in which he had arranged the drapery, it went to my heart to take it down, and suspend in its place some pretty blue linen curtains which I had brought from the valley. My toilet table is formed of a trunk elevated upon two claret cases, and by draping it with some more of the blue linen neatly fringed, it really will look quite handsome, and when I have placed upon it my rosewood workbox, a large cushion of crimson brocade, some Chinese ornaments of exquisitely carved ivory, and two or three Bohemian glass cologne stands, it would not disgrace a lady's chamber at home.

The looking-glass is one of those which come in paper cases for doll's houses; how different from the full length

Psyches so almost indispensible to a dressing-room in the States.

The wash-stand is another trunk covered with a towel, upon which you will see for bowl, a large vegetable dish, for ewer, a common sized dining pitcher; near this, upon a small cask, is placed a pail, which is daily filled with water from the river. I brought with me from Marysville a handsome carpet, a hair mattress, pillows, a profusion of bed linen, quilts, blankets, towels, &c., so that in spite of the oddity of most of my furniture, I am in reality as thoroughly comfortable here as I could be in the most elegant palace.

We have four chairs which were brought from the Empire. I seriously proposed having three-legged stools; with my usual desire for symmetry I thought that they would be more in keeping; but as I was told that it would be a great deal of trouble to get them made, I was fain to put up with mere chairs; so you see that even in the land of gold itself, one cannot have everything that she desires. An ingenious individual in the neighborhood, blessed with a large bump for mechanics and good nature, made me a sort of wide bench, which covered with a neat plaid, looks quite sofa-like. A little pine table with oil-cloth tacked over the top of it, stands in one corner of the room, upon which is arranged the chess and cribbage boards. There is a larger one for dining purposes, and as unpainted pine has always a most dreary look, F. went every where in search of oil-cloth for it, but there was none on any of the bars; at last "Ned," the Humboldt Paganini, remembered two old monte table covers, which had been thrown aside as useless. I received them thankfully, and with my planning and Ned's mechanical genius, we patched up quite a respectable covering; to be sure, the ragged condition of the

primitive material, compelled us to have at one end an
extra border, but that only agreeably relieved the monotony. I must mention that the floor is so uneven that no
article of furniture gifted with four legs pretends to stand
upon but three at once, so that the chairs, tables, etc., remind you constantly of a dog with a sore foot.

At each end of the mantle-piece is arranged a candlestick, not, much to my regret, a block of wood with a hole
in the centre of it, but a real brittania-ware candlestick;
the space between is gaily ornamented with F.'s meer-
schaum, several styles of clay pipes, cigars, cigaritos, and
every procurable variety of tobacco; for you know the
aforesaid individual is a perfect devotee of the Indian
weed. If I should give you a month of Sundays you would
never guess what we use in lieu of a bookcase, so I will put
you out of your misery by informing you instantly that it
is nothing more nor less than a candle-box, which contains
the library, consisting of a bible and prayer-book,
Shakespeare, Spenser, Coleridge, Shelley, Keats, Lowell's
Fable for Critics, Walton's Complete Angler and some
Spanish books—spiritual instead of material lights, you
see.

There, my dainty Lady Molly, I have given you, I fear, a
wearisomely minute description of my new home. How
would you like to winter in such an abode? in a place
where there are no newspapers, no churches, lectures,
concerts or theaters; no fresh books, no shopping, calling
nor gossiping little tea-drinkings; no parties, no balls, no
picnics, no *tableaux*, no charades, no latest fashions, no
daily mail, (we have an express once a month,) no prom-
enades, no rides nor drives; no vegetables but potatoes and
onions, no milk, no eggs, no *nothing*? Now I expect to be
very happy here. This strange, odd life, fascinates me. As
for churches, "the groves were God's first temples," "and

for the strength of the hills, the Swiss mountains bless
him;'' and as to books, I read Shakespeare, David,
Spenser, Paul, Coleridge, Burns and Shelley which are
never old. In good sooth I fancy that nature intended me
for an Arab or some other Nomadic barbarian, and by mistake my soul got packed up in a christianized set of bones
and muscles. How I shall ever be able to content myself to
live in a decent, proper, well-behaved house, where toilet
tables are toilet tables, and not an ingenious combination
of trunk and claret cases, where lanterns are not broken
bottles, book cases not candle boxes, and trunks not
wash-stands, but every article of furniture, instead of
being a make-shift, is its own useful and elegantly finished
self. I am sure I do not know, however, when too much
appalled at the humdrumish prospect, I console myself
with the beautiful promises, "that sufficient unto the day
is the evil thereof," and "as thy day is, so shall thy
strength be," and trust that when it is again my lot to live
amid the refinements and luxuries of civilization, that I
shall endure them with becoming philosophy and for-
titude.

LETTER EIGHTH

A TRIP INTO THE MINES

From our Log Cabin, Indian Bar,
October 20, 1851

HAVING SEEN me, dear M., safely enthroned in my beautiful log palace, with its center walls all tapestried with moss, perhaps you would like a description of the coronation dinner!

You must know that "Ned," the Paganini of the Humboldt, (who, by the way, is almost a historic: or better, perhaps, naval character, inasmuch as he was *cook* on board of the Somers, when her captain performed his little tragedy, to the horror of an entire nation,) had been in such a state of ecstasy ever since he had heard of the promised advent of Mrs.———, that his *proprietors*, as Ned grandly calls them, had serious fears of being compelled to strait jacket him.

"You see, sir," said Ned, "when the queen (with Ned as with the rest of the world, 'a substitute shines brightly as a queen, until a queen be by,' and I am the only petticoated astonishment on this Bar) arrives, *she* will appreciate my culinary efforts. It is really discouraging, sir, after I have exhausted my skill in preparing a dish, to see the gentlemen devour it with as much unconcern, as though it had been cooked by a mere bungler in our art!"

When we entered our new home, we found the cloth—it was a piece left of that which lined the room overhead— already laid. As it was unhemmed and somewhat tattered at the ends, an imaginative mind might fancy it fringed on purpose, though like the poor little "Marchioness," with

her orange peel and water, one "would have to *make believe* very hard." Unfortunately, it was not wide enough
for the table, and a dashing border of white pine banded
each side of it. Ned had invested an unknown quantity of
gold-dust in a yard of diaper—awfully coarse—which, divided into four pieces, and fringed, to match the table
cloth, he had placed napkin-wise in the tumblers. He had
evidently ransacked the whole Bar to get viands wherewith to decorate the various dishes, which were as follows—

    First Course—Oyster Soup.
    Second Course—Fried Salmon, caught from the river.
    Third Course—Roast Beef and Boiled Ham.
    Fourth Course—Fried Oysters.
    Vegetables—Potatoes and Onions.
    Pastry—Mince Pie, and Pudding, made without eggs or
milk.
    Dessert—Madeira Nuts and Raisins.
    Wines—Claret and Champagne.
    Coffee.

I found that Ned had not overrated his powers; the dinner, when one considers the materials of which it was
composed, was really excellent. The soup was truly a great
work of art; the fried oysters dreamily delicious; and as to
the coffee, Ned must have got the receipt for making it
from the very angel who gave the beverage to Mahomet, to
restore that individual's decayed moisture.
    Ned himself waited, dressed in a brand new flannel shirt
and calico ditto, his hair—he is a light mulatto—frizzled to
the most intense degree of corkscrewity, and a benign and
self-satisfied smile irradiating his face, such as *should* il-
lumine the features of a great artist, when he knows that

he has achieved something, the memory of which the world will not willingly let die. In truth he needed but white kid gloves, to have been worthy of standing behind the chair of Count D'Orsay himself. So grand was his air, so ceremonious his every motion, that we forgot we were living in the heart of the Sierra Nevada; forgot that our home was a log cabin of mere primitive rudeness; forgot that we were sitting at a rough pine table, covered with a ragged piece of four cent cotton cloth, eating soup with iron spoons!

I wish, my funny little Molly, that you could have been here, clairvoyantly. It was one of those scenes just touched with that fine and almost imperceptible *perfume* of the ludicrous, in which you especially delight. There are a thousand minute shreds of the absurd, which my duller sense overlooks, but which never can hope to escape your mirth loving vision.

Ned really plays beautifully on the violin. There is a white man by the name of "Chock," who generally accompanies him. Of course, true daughter of Eve that you are, you will wish to know "right off" what "Chock's" *other* name is. Young woman, I am ashamed of you! Who ever asks for the *other* name of Alexander, of Hannibal, of Homer? Suffice it that he is "Chock" by himself, "Chock" and assistant violinist to Paganini Vattal Ned.

Ned and one of his musical cronies, a white man, gave me a serenade the other evening. As it was quite cold, F. made them come inside the cabin. It was the richest thing possible, to see the patronizing, and yet serene manner, with which Ned directed his companion what marches, preludes, etc., to play for the amusement of that profound culinary and musical critic, "Dame Shirley."

It must be confessed that Ned's love of the beautiful is not quite so correct, as his taste in cooking and violin playing. This morning a gentle knock at my door, was followed by that polite person, bearing in triumph a small waiter, purloined from the Humboldt, on which stood in state, festooned with tumblers, a gaudy pitcher, which would have thrown "Tearsoul" and "Lelie" into ecstasies of delight. It was almost as wonderful a specimen of art as my chintz hanging. The ground-work is pure white, upon which in bas relief are *executed* two diabolical looking bandits, appallingly bewhiskered and mustached; dressed in red coats, yellow pantaloons, green boots, orange colored caps, with brown feathers in them, and sky-blue bows and arrows—each of the fascinating vagabonds is attended by a bird of paradise colored dog, with a crimson tail waggingly depicted. They are embowered beneath a morning-glory vine, evidently a species of the convolvulus unknown in America, as each one of its pink leaves springing from purple stems, is three times the size of the bandit's head.

Ned could not have admired it more, if it had been a jar of richest porcelain or the rare Etruscan vase, and when I gently suggested that it was a pity to rob the bar-room of so elegant an ornament, answered,

"Miners can't appreciate a handsome pitcher, any more than they can good cooking, and Mrs.——— will please to keep it."

Alas! I would infinitely have preferred the humblest brown jug, for that really *has* a certain beauty of its own, and besides it would have been in keeping with my cabin. However, that good creature looked upon the miraculous vegetable, the fabulous quadrupeds, and the impossible bipeds, with so much pride, that I had not the heart to tell him that the pitcher was a fright, but graciously accepting it, I hid it out of sight as quick as possible, on the trunk washstand, behind the curtain.

We breakfast at nine, and dine at six, with a dish of soup at noon for luncheon. Do not think we fare as sumptuously *every* day, as we did at the coronation dinner. By no means; and it is said that there will probably be many weeks during the season, that we shall have neither onions, potatoes nor fresh meat. It is feared that the former will not keep through the whole winter, and the rancheros cannot at all times drive in cattle for butchering, on account of the expected snow.

Ned is not the only distinguished person residing on this Bar. There is a man camping here, who was one of Colonel Fremont's guides during his travels through California. He is fifty years of age, perhaps, and speaks several languages to perfection. As he has been a wanderer for many years, and for a long time was the principal chief of the Crow Indians, his adventures are extremely interesting. He chills the blood of the green young miner, who, unacquainted with the arts of war and subjugation, congregate around him by the cold blooded manner in which he relates the Indian fights that he has been engaged in.

There is quite a band of this wild people herding a few miles below us; and soon after my arrival it was confidently affirmed and believed by many, that they were about to make a murderous attack upon the miners. This man who can make himself understood in almost any language, and has a great deal of influence over all Indians, went to see them and told them that such an attempt would result in their own certain destruction. They said "that they had never thought of such a thing; that the Americans were like the grass in the valleys, and the Indians fewer than the flowers of the Sierra Nevada."

Among other oddities, there is a person here who is a rabid admirer of Lippard. I have heard him gravely affirm that Lippard was the greatest author the world ever saw,

and that if one of his novels, and the most fascinating
work of ancient or modern times, lay side by side, he
would choose the former, even though he had already repeatedly perused it. He *studies* Lippard just as other folks
do Shakespeare, and yet the man has read and *admires* the
majestic prose of Chilton, and is quite familiar with the
best English classics! He is a Quaker and his merciless and
unmitigated regard for truth, is comically grand, and
nothing amuses me more than to draw out that peculiar
characteristic. For instance, after talking *at* him, the most
beautiful and eloquent things that I can think of, I will
pitilessly nail him in this wise—

"Now I know that *you* agree with me, Mr.———?"

It is the richest and broadest farce, in this flattering and
deceitful world, to see him look right into my eyes, while
he answers smilingly, without the least evasion or reserve,
the astounding *truth*—

"I have not heard a word that you have been saying for
the last half hour; I have been thinking of something
else!"

His dreamland reveries on these occasions are supposed
to be a profound meditation upon the character and writ-
ings of his pet author. I am always glad to have him visit
us, as some one of us is sure to be most unflatteringly elec-
trified by his uncompromising veracity. I am myself generally the victim, as I make it a point to give him every
opportunity for the display of this unusual peculiarity.
Not but that I have had disagreeable truth told me often
enough, but heretofore people have done it out of spite-
fulness; but Mr.———, who is the kindest hearted of mortals, never dreams that his merciless frankness, can possibly wound one's self-love.

But *the* great man—officially considered—of the entire
river, is the "Squire," as he is jestingly called. It had been

rumored for some time, that we were about to become a
law and order loving community; and when I requested an
explanation, I was informed that a man had gone all the
way to Hamilton, the county seat, to get himself made
into a Justice of the Peace. Many shook their wise heads
and doubted—even if suited to the situation, which they
say he is not—whether he would *take* here; and certain
rebel spirits affirmed that he would be invited to *walk
over the hill* before he had been in the community twenty-
four hours; which is a polite way these free-and-easy
young people have, of turning out of town an obnoxious
individual. Not that the "Squire" is particularly objec-
tionable, *per se*, but in virtue of his office, and his supposed ineligibility to fill the same. Besides, the people
here wish to have the fun of ruling themselves. Miners are
as fond of playing at law-making and dispensing, as
French novelists are of "playing at Providence." They say,
also, that he was not elected by the voice of the people,
but that his personal friends nominated and voted for him
unknown to the rest of the community. This is, perhaps,
true. At least I have heard some of the most respectable
men here observe, that had they been aware of the
Squire's name being up as candidate for an office, which
though insignificant elsewhere, is one of great responsibility in a mining community, they should certainly have
gone against his election.

Last night I had the honor of an introduction to "*His*
Honor." Imagine a middle-sized man, quite stout, with a
head disproportionately large, crowned with one of those
immense foreheads eked out with a slight baldness (wonder if according to the flattering popular superstition, he
has *thought* his hair off?) which enchant phrenologists,
but which one *never* sees brooding above the soulful orbs
of the great ones of the earth; a smooth, fat face, grey eyes

and prominent chin, the *tout ensemble* characterized by
an expression of the utmost meekness and gentleness,
which expression contrasts rather funnily with a satanic
goatee, and you have our good "Squire."

You know, M., that it takes the same *kind* of power—
differing of course in degree—to govern twenty men that
it does to rule a million, and although the "Squire" is suf-
ficiently intelligent and the kindest hearted creature in
the world, he evidently does *not* possess that peculiar tact,
talent, gift or whatever it is called, which makes Napo-
leons, Mohammeds and Cromwells, and which is absolutely necessary to keep in order such a strangely amalga-
mated community, representing as it does the four quarters of the globe, as congregates upon this river.

However, I suppose that we must take the "goods the
Gods provide," satisfied that if our "King Log" does no
good; he is too sincerely desirous of fulfilling his duty, to
do any harm. But I really feel sorry for this "mere young
Daniel come to judgment," when I think of the gauntlet
which the wicked wits will make him run when he tries his
first cause.

However, the "Squire" may, after all, succeed. As yet
he has had no opportunity of making use of his credentials
in putting down Miner's Law, which is of course the famous code of Judge Lynch. In the mean time, we all sincerely pray that he may be successful in his laudable undertaking, for justice in the hands of a mob, however respectable, is at best a fearful thing.

LETTER NINTH

A TRIP INTO THE MINES

From our Log Cabin, Indian Bar,
October 29, 1851

WELL, MY dear M., our grand "Squire," whom I sketched for you in my last letter, has at length had an opportunity to exercise (or rather to *try* to do so) his judicial power upon a criminal case. His first appearance as Justice of the Peace, took place a week ago, and was caused, I think, by a prosecution for debt. On that momentous occasion, the proceeding having been carried on in the bar-room of the Empire, it is said that our "Young Daniel" stopped the court twice in order to treat the jury!

But let me tell you about the trial which has just taken place. On Sunday evening last, Ned Paganini rushing wildly up to our cabin, and with eyes so enormously dilated that they absolutely looked *all* white, exclaimed, "that 'Little John' had been arrested for stealing four hundred dollars from the proprietor of the Empire; and that he was at that very moment undergoing an examination before the 'Squire,' in the bar-room of the Humboldt, where he was apprehended while betting at monte." "And," added Ned, with a most awe-inspiring shake of his cork-screws, "there is no doubt but that he will be hung!"

Of course I was inexpressibly shocked at Ned's news, for "Little John," as he is always called, (who, by the way, is about the last person—as every one remarked—that would have been suspected), seemed quite like an acquaintance, as he was waiter at the Empire when I boarded there. I hurried F. off as quickly as possible, to inquire into the truth of the report. He soon returned with the following particulars:

It seems that Mr. B. who on Sunday morning wished to pay a bill, on taking his purse from between the two mattresses of the bed whereon he was accustomed to sleep, which stood in the common sitting-room of the family, found that four hundred dollars in gold dust was missing. He did not for one moment suspect "Little John," in whom himself and wife had always placed the utmost confidence—until a man who happened to be in the bar-room towards evening, mentioned casually "that 'Little John' was then at the Humboldt betting," or to speak technically,—" 'bucking' away large sums at monte." Mr. B., who knew that he had no money of his own, immediately came over to Indian Bar and had him arrested upon suspicion. Although he had lost several ounces, he had still about a hundred dollars remaining. But as it is impossible to identify gold-dust, Mr. B. could not swear that the money was his.

Of course, the prisoner loudly protested his innocence; and as he was very drunk, the "Squire" adjourned all further proceedings until the next day—placing him under keepers for the night.

On the following morning I was awakened very early by a tremendous "aye"—so deep and mighty that it almost seemed to shake the cabin with its thrilling emphasis. I sprang up and ran to the window, but could *see* nothing, of course—as our house stands behind the Humboldt; but I could easily understand from the confused murmur of many voices, and the rapidly succeeding "ayes" and "noes," that a large crowd had collected in front of the latter. My first apprehension was expressed by my bursting into tears and exclaiming—

"Oh! F., for God's sake rise; the mob are going to hang 'Little John!' "

And my fear was not so absurd as you might at first imagine, for men have often been executed in the mines, for stealing a much smaller sum than four hundred dollars.

F. went to the Humboldt and returned in a few minutes to tell me that I might stop weeping, for John was going to have a regular trial. The crowd was merely a miners' meeting, called by Mr. B. for the purpose of having the trial held at the Empire for the convenience of his wife, who could not walk over to Indian Bar to give her evidence in the case. However, as her deposition could easily have been taken, malicious people *will* say that it was for the convenience of her husband's *pockets*—as it was well known that at whichever house the trial took place, the owners thereof would make a handsome profit from the sale of dinners, drinks, etc., to the large number of people who would congregate to witness the proceedings. Miners are proverbial for their reverence to the sex. Of course, everything ought to yield where a lady is concerned, and they all very properly agreed *nem con*, to Mr. B.'s request.

The "Squire" consented to hold the court at Rich Bar, although many think that thereby he compromised his judicial dignity, as his office is on Indian Bar. I must confess I see not how he could have done otherwise. The miners were only too ready (so much do they object to a Justice of the Peace) to take the case *entirely* out of his hands, if their wishes were not complied with; which, to confess the truth, they *did*, even after all his concessions! though they *pretended* to keep up a sort of mock respect for his office.

Everybody went to Rich Bar. No one remained to protect the calico shanties, the rag huts and the log cabins,

from the much talked of Indian attack—but your humble
servant and Paganini Ned.

When the people, the mighty people, had assembled at
the Empire, they commenced proceedings by voting in a
president and jury of their own; though they kindly consented (how *very* condescending!) that the "Squire"
might *play at judge*, by sitting at the side of *their* elected
magistrate! This honor, the "Squire" seemed to take as a
sort of salvo to his wounded dignity, and with unprece-
dented meekness *accepted* it. A young Irishman from St.
Louis was appointed counsel for John, and a Dr. C. acted
for the prosecution,—neither of them, however, were
lawyers.

The evidence against the prisoner was: that he had no
money previously; that he had slept at the Empire a night
or two before; and that he knew where Mr. B. was in the
habit of keeping his gold dust; with a few other circumstances equally unimportant. His only defense was, of
course to account for the money, which he tried to do by
the following ingenious story:

He said that his father, who resides at Stockholm (he is
a Swede) had sent him two months previously, five hundred dollars through the express, which had been brought
to him from San Francisco by a young man whose name is
Miller; that he told no one of the circumstance, but buried
the money (a common habit with the miner) on the summit of a hill about half a mile from Indian Bar; that being
intoxicated on Sunday morning, he had dug it up for the
purpose of gambling with it; and that Mr. M. who had
gone to Marysville a week before, and would return in a
fortnight, could confirm his story. When asked if he had
received a letter with the money, he replied that he did;
but having placed it between the lining and the top of his

cap, he had unfortunately lost it. He earnestly affirmed his innocence, and through his counsel, entreated the Court, should he be condemned, to defer the execution of his sentence until the arrival of Miller, by whom he could prove all that he had stated. Notwithstanding the florid eloquence of W., the jury brought in a verdict of guilty, and condemned him to receive thirty-nine lashes at nine o'clock the following morning, and to leave the river, never to return to it, within twenty-four hours; a "claim" of which he owned a part, to be made over to Mr. B., to indemnify him for his loss. His punishment was very light on account of his previous popularity and inoffensive conduct. In spite of his really ingenious defense, no one has the least doubt of his guilt, but his lawyer and the "Squire;" they as firmly believe him an innocent and much injured man.

Yesterday morning I made my visit to Smith's Bar. In order to reach it, it was necessary to cross the river, on a bridge formed of two logs, to Missouri Bar. This flat, which has been worked but very little, has a path leading across it, a quarter of a mile in length. It contains but two or three huts, no very extensive "diggings," having as yet been discovered upon it. About in the middle of it, and close to the side of the trail, is situated a burial spot, where, not only its dead repose, but those who die on Indian Bar are also brought for interment. On arriving at the termination of the level, another log bridge leads to Smith's Bar, which, although it lies upon the same side of the river as our settlement, is seldom approached, as I before observed, except by crossing to Missouri Bar and back again from that to Smith's. The hills rise so perpendicularly between this latter and Indian Bar that it is utterly impossible for a woman to follow on the trail along their side, and it is no child's play for even the most hardy mountaineer to do it.

This level (Smith's Bar) is large and quite thickly settled. More gold has been taken from it than from any
other settlement on the river. Although the scenery here is
not so strikingly picturesque as that surrounding my new
home, it is perhaps more lovely; and certainly infinitely
more desirable as a place of residence than the latter, because the sun shines upon it all winter, and we can take
long walks about it in many directions. Now, Indian Bar is
so completely covered with excavations and tenements,
that it is utterly impossible to promenade upon it at all.
Whenever I wish for exercise, I am *compelled* to cross the
river, which, of course, I cannot do without company;—
and as the latter is not always procurable (F.'s profession
calling him much from home) I am obliged to stay in
doors more than I like or is conducive to my health.

A short, but steep ascent from Smith's Bar leads you to
another "bench" (as miners call it) almost as large as itself,
which is covered with trees and grass, and is a most lovely
place. From here, one has a charming view of a tiny bar
called Frenchman's. It is a most sunny little spot, covered
with the freshest greensward, and nestling lovingly, like a
petted darling, in the embracing curve of a crescent-
shaped hill opposite. It looks more like some sheltered
nook amid the blue mountains of New England, than anything I have ever yet seen in California. Formerly there
was a "Deer Lick" upon it; and I am told that on every
dewy morning or starlit evening, you might see a herd of
pretty creatures, gathering in antlered beauty about its
margin.

Now, however, they are seldom met with; the advent of
gold-hunting humanity having driven them far up into the
hills.

The man who keeps the store at which we stopped (a
log cabin without any floor) goes by the *sobriquet* of
"Yank," and is quite a character in his way. He used to be

a peddler in the States, and is remarkable for an intense ambition to be thought what the Yankees call "cute and smart;" an ambition which his true and good heart will never permit him to achieve. He is a great friend of mine (I am always interested in that *bizarre* mixture of shrewdness and simplicity of which he is a distinguishing specimen) and takes me largely into his confidence, as to the various ways he has of *doing* green miners. All the merest delusion on his part, you understand—for he is the most honest of God's creatures, and would not, I verily believe, cheat a man out of a grain of golden sand to save his own harmless and inoffensive life. He is popularly supposed to be smitten with the charms of the "Indiana Girl;" but I confess I doubt it, for "Yank" himself informed me confidentially, that "though a very superior and splendid woman, she had no *polish!*"

He is an indefatigable "snapper-up of unconsidered trifles," and his store is the most comical *olla podrida* of heterogeneous merchandise that I ever saw. There is nothing you can ask for but what he has,—from crowbars down to cambric needles; from velveteen trowsers up to broadcloth coats of the jauntiest description. The *quality* of his goods, it must be confessed, is sometimes rather equivocal. His collection of novels is by far the largest, the greasiest, and the "yellowest kivered" of any to be found on the river. I will give you an instance of the variety of his possessions.

I wanted some sealing-wax to mend a broken chesspiece, having, by some strange carelessness, left the box containing mine in Marysville. I inquired everywhere for it, but always got laughed at for supposing that any one would be so absurd as to bring such an article into the mountains. As a forlorn hope I applied to "Yank." Of course, he had plenty! The best of it is, that whenever he produces any of these out-of-the-way things, he always says that he brought them from the States;—which proves that he had a remarkable degree of foresight, when he left his home three years ago!

While I sat chatting with "Yank," I heard some one singing loudly, and apparently very gaily, a negro melody; and the next moment, who should enter but "Little John," who had been whipped according to sentence, three hours previously. As soon as he saw me, he burst into tears, and exclaimed—

"Oh! Mrs.———, a heartless mob has beaten me cruelly, has taken all my money from me, and has decreed that I, who am an innocent man, should leave the mountains, without a cent of money to assist me on my way!"

The latter part of his speech, as I afterwards discovered, was *certainly* a lie;—for he knew that a sum amply sufficient to pay his expenses to Marysville had been subscribed by the very people who believed him guilty. Of course, his complaints were extremely painful to me. You know how weakly pitiful I always am towards wicked people;—for it seems to me, that they are so much more to be compassionated than the good.

But what *could* I say to poor John? I did not for one moment doubt his entire guilt; and so, as people often do on such occasions, I took refuge in a platitude.

"Well, John," I sagely remarked, "I hope that you did not take the money. And only think how much happier you are in that case, than if you had been beaten and abused as you say you have, and at the same time were a criminal!"

I must confess, much as it tells against my eloquence, that John did not receive my well-meant attempt at consolation, with that pious gratitude, which such an injured innocent ought to have exhibited; but F. luckily calling me at that moment, I was spared any more of his tearful complaints.

Soon after our return to the cabin, John's lawyer and the "Squire" called upon us. They declared their perfect conviction of his innocence; and the latter remarked, that if any one would accompany him, he would walk up to the spot and examine the hole from whence the culprit affirmed that he had taken his money, only three days ago;—as he very naturally supposed that it would still exhibit signs of having been recently opened. It was finally agreed that the victim, who had never described the place to the Squire, should give a minute description of it—unheard by his Honor—to F.; and afterwards should lead the former, accompanied by his counsel (no one else could be persuaded to make such martyrs of themselves) to the much-talked-of spot. And will you believe it, M., those two obstinate men actually persevered, although it was nearly dark and a very cold, raw, windy night, in walking half a mile, up one of the steepest hills, on what the rest thought a perfect fool's errand! To be sure, they have triumphed for the moment, for the "Squire's" description on their return, tallied exactly with that previously given to F. But alas! the infidels remained infidels still.

Then W. bet an oyster supper for the whole party, which F. took up, that Miller on his return would confirm his client's statement. For fear of accidents we had the oysters that night, and very nice they were, I assure you. This morning the hero of the last three days vanished to parts unknown. And thus endeth the "Squire's" first attempt to sit in judgment on a criminal case. I regret his failure very much, as do many others. Whether any one else could have succeeded better, I cannot say. But I am sure that no person could more sincerely *desire* and *try* to act for the best good of the community than the "Squire."

I suppose that I should be as firm a believer in John's innocence as any one, had he not said to F. and others, that "If he had taken the money they could not *prove* it against him;" and many other similar things, which seem to me totally incompatible with innocence.

A TRIP INTO THE MINES

From our Log Cabin, Indian Bar,
November 25, 1851

NOTHING OF importance has happened since I last
wrote you, except that I have become a *mineress;* that is,
if the having washed a pan of dirt with my own hands, and
procured therefrom three dollars and twenty-five cents in
gold dust, (which I shall inclose in this letter), will entitle
me to the name. I can truly say, with the blacksmith's ap-
prentice at the close of his first day's work at the anvil,
that "I am sorry I learned the trade;" for I wet my feet,
tore my dress, spoilt a pair of new gloves, nearly froze my
fingers, got an awful headache, took cold and lost a valuable breastpin, in this my labor of love. After such melancholy self-sacrifice on my part, I trust you will duly prize
my gift. I can assure you that it is the last golden handiwork you will ever receive from "Dame Shirley."

Apropos, of lady gold-washers in general,—it is a common habit with people residing in towns in the vicinity of
the "Diggings," to make up pleasure parties to those
places. Each woman of the company will exhibit on her
return, at least twenty dollars of the *oro*, which she will
gravely inform you she has just "panned out" from a single basinful of the soil. This, of course, gives strangers a

very erroneous idea of the average richness of auriferous
dirt. I myself thought, (now don't laugh,) that one had
but to saunter gracefully along romantic streamlets, on
sunny afternoons, with a parasol and white kid gloves,
perhaps, and to stop now and then to admire the scenery,
and carelessly rinse out a small panful of yellow sand,
(without detriment to the white kids, however, so easy
did I fancy the whole process to be), in order to fill one's
workbag with the most beautiful and rare specimens of
the precious mineral. Since I have been here, I have discovered my mistake, and also the secret of the brilliant success of former gold-washeresses.

The miners are in the habit of flattering the vanity of
their fair visitors, by scattering a handful of "salt" (which,
strange to say, is *exactly* the color of gold dust, and has
the remarkable property of often bringing to light very
curious lumps of the ore) through the dirt before the
dainty fingers touch it; and the dear creatures go home
with their treasures, firmly believing that mining is the
prettiest pastime in the world.

I had no idea of permiting such a costly joke to be
played upon me; so I said but little of my desire to "go
through the motions" of gold washing, until one day,
when, as I passed a deep hole in which several men were at
work, my companion requested the owner to fill a small
pan, which I had in my hand, with dirt from the bedrock.
This request was, of course, granted, and, the treasure having been conveyed to the edge of the river, I succeeded,
after much awkward maneuvering on my own part, and
considerable assistance from friend H., an experienced
miner, in gathering together the above specified sum. All
the diggers of our acquaintance say that it is an excellent
"prospect," even to come from the bedrock, where,
naturally, the richest dirt is found. To be sure, there are

now and then "lucky strikes"; such, for instance, as that mentioned in a former letter, where a person took out of a single basinful of soil, two hundred and fifty-six dollars. But such luck is as rare as the winning of a hundred thousand dollar prize in a lottery. We are acquainted with many here whose gains have *never* amounted to much more than "wages"; that is, from six to eight dollars a day. And a "claim" which yields a man a steady income of ten dollars *per diem*, is considered as very valuable.

I received an immense fright the other morning. I was sitting by the fire, quietly reading "Lewis Arundal," which had just fallen into my hands, when a great shout and trampling of feet outside attracted my attention. Naturally enough my first impulse was to run to the door; but scarcely had I risen to my feet for that purpose, when a mighty crash against the side of the cabin, shaking it to the foundation, threw me suddenly upon my knees. So violent was the shock, that for a moment I thought the staunch old logs, mossed with the pale verdure of ages, were falling in confusion around me. As soon as I could collect my scattered senses, I looked about to see what had happened. Several stones had fallen from the back of the chimney, mortar from the latter covered the hearth, the cloth overhead was twisted into the funniest possible wrinkles, the couch had jumped two feet from the side of the house, the little table lay on its back holding up *four* legs instead of *one*, the chessmen were rolling merrily about in every direction, the dishes had all left their usual places, the door, which ever since has obstinately refused to let itself be shut, was thrown violently open, while an odd looking pile of articles lay in the middle of the room, which, upon investigation, was found to consist of a pail, a broom, a bell, some candlesticks, a pack of cards, a loaf of bread, a pair of boots, a bunch of cigars, and some clay

pipes—the only things, by the way, rendered utterly *hors
de combat* in the assault. But one piece of furniture retained its attitude, and that was the elephantine bedstead,
which nothing short of an earthquake could move. Almost at the same moment several acquaintances rushed in,
begging me not to be alarmed, as the danger was past.

"But what has happened?" I eagerly inquired.

"Oh, a large tree which was felled this morning, has
rolled down from the brow of the hill," and its having
struck a rock a few feet from the house, losing thereby the
most of its force, had alone saved us from utter destruction.

I grew sick with terror when I understood the awful
fate from which Providence had preserved me; and even
now my heart leaps painfully with mingled fear and gratitude, when I think how closely that pale death shadow
glided by me, and of the loving care which forbade it to
linger upon our threshold.

Every one who saw the forest giant descending the hill
with the force of a mighty torrent, expected to see the
cabin instantly prostrated to the earth. As it was, they all
say that it swayed from the perpendicular more than six
inches.

Poor W.—whom you may remember my having mentioned in a former letter as having had a leg amputated, a
few weeks ago, and who was visiting us at the time, (he
had been brought from the Empire in a rocking chair),
looked like a marble statue of resignation. He possesses a
face of uncommon beauty, and his large, dark eyes have
always, I fancy, a sorrowful expression. Although he
knew from the first shout what was about to happen, and
was sitting on the couch which stood at the side of the
cabin where the log must necessarily strike, and in his
mutilated condition, had, as he has since said, not the

faintest hope of escape, yet the rich color, for which he is remarkable, paled not a shade during the whole affair.

The woodman, who came so near causing a catastrophe, was, I believe, infinitely more frightened than his might-have-been victims. He is a good natured, stupid creature, and did not dare to descend the hill until some time after the excitement had subsided. The ludicrous expression of terror which his countenance wore, when he came in to see what damage had been done, and to ask pardon for his carelessness, made us all laugh heartily.

W. related the almost miraculous escape of two persons from a similar danger last winter. The cabin, which was on Smith's Bar, was crushed into a mass of ruins almost in an instant; while an old man and his daughter, who were at dinner within its walls, remained sitting in the midst of the fallen logs, entirely unhurt. The father immediately seized a gun and ran after the careless woodman, swearing that he would shoot him. Fortunately for the latter (for there is no doubt that in the first moments of his rage the old man would have slain him) his younger legs enabled him to make his escape, and he did not dare to return to the settlement for some days.

It has heretofore been a source of great interest to me to listen to the ringing sound of the axe, and the solemn crash of those majestic sentinels of the hills, as they bow their green foreheads to the dust; but now I fear that I shall always hear them with a feeling of apprehension, mingling with my former awe, although every one tells us that there is no danger of a repetition of the accident.

Last week there was a *post mortem* examination of two men who died very suddenly in the neighborhood. Perhaps it will sound rather barbarous, when I tell you that, as there was no building upon the Bar which admitted light enough for the purpose, it was found necessary to conduct the examination in the open air, to the intense interest of the Kanakas, Indians, French, Spanish, English, Irish and Yankees, who had gathered eagerly about the spot. Paganini Ned, with an anxious desire that Mrs.——— should be *amused* as much as possible in her mountain home, rushed up from the kitchen, his dusky face radiant with excitement, to inform me "that I could see both the bodies by just looking out of the window!" I really frightened the poor fellow by the abrupt and vehement manner in which I declined taking advantage of his kindly hint.

One of the deceased, was the husband of an American lady-lecturess of the most intense description, and a strong-minded "Bloomer" on the broadest principles.

Apropos, how *can* women,—many of whom, I am told, are *really* interesting and intelligent, how *can* they spoil their pretty mouths and ruin their beautiful complexions, by demanding with Xantippean *fervor*, in the presence, often, of a vulgar, irreverent mob, what the gentle creatures, are pleased to call their "rights?" How *can* they wish to soil the delicate texture of their airy fancies, by pondering over the wearying stupidities of Presidential elections, or the bewildering mystifications of rabid metaphysicians? And, above all, how *can* they so far forget the sweet, shy coquetries of shrinking womanhood, as to don those horrid "Bloomers?" As for me, although a *wife*, I never wear the—————, well you know what they call them, when they wish to quiz henpecked husbands,—even in the strictest privacy of life. I confess to an almost religious veneration for trailing drapery, and I pin my vestural faith with unflinching obstinacy to sweeping petticoats.

I knew a "strong-minded Bloomer," at home, of some talent, and who was possessed, in a certain sense, of an excellent education. One day, after having flatteringly informed me, that I really *had* a "soul above buttons" and the nursery, she gravely proposed that I should improve my *mind*, by poring six hours a day over the metaphysical subleties of Kant, Cousin, &c; and I remember, that she called me a "piece of fashionable insipidity," and taunted me with not daring to go out of the beaten track, because I *truly* thought, (for in those days I was a humble little thing enough, and sincerely desirous of walking in the right path as straightly as my feeble judgment would permit,) that there were other authors, more congenial to the flower-like delicacy of the feminine intellect than her pet writers.

When will our sex appreciate the exquisite philosophy and truth of Lowell's remark upon the habits of Lady Red-Breast and her *sposa* Robin, as illustrating the beautifully-varied spheres of man and woman:—

"He sings to the wide world, she to her nest;
In the nice ear of Nature, which song is the best?"

Speaking of birds, reminds me of a misfortune that I have lately experienced, which, in a life where there is so little to amuse and interest one, has been to me a subject of real grief. About three weeks ago, F. saw on the hill, a California pheasant, which he chased into a coyote hole and captured. Knowing how fond I am of pets, he brought it home and proposed that I should try to tame it. Now from earliest childhood, I have resolutely refused to keep *wild* birds, and when I have had them given to me—which has happened several times in this country—young blue-birds, etc.,—I have invariably set them free; and I proposed doing the same with the pretty pheasant; but as they are the most delicately exquisite in flavor of all game,

F. said "that if I did not wish to keep it, he would wring its neck and have it served up for dinner." With the cruelty of kindness, often more disastrous than that of real malice, I shrank from having it killed, and consented to let it run about the cabin.

It was a beautiful bird, a little larger than the domestic hen. Its slender neck, which it curved with haughty elegance, was tinted with various shades of a shining steel color. The large, bright eye glanced with the prettiest shyness at its captors, and the cluster of feathers forming its tail, drooped with the rare grace of an ostrich-plume. The colors of the body were of a subdued brilliancy, reminding one of a rich but somber mosiac.

As it seemed very quiet, I really believed that in time we should be able to tame it—still it *would* remain constantly under the sofa or bedstead; so F. concluded to place it in a cage, for a few hours of each day, in order that it might become gradually accustomed to our presence. This was done, the bird appearing as well as ever; and after closing the door of its temporary prison one day, I left it and returned to my seat by the fire. In less than two minutes afterwards, a slight struggle in the cage, attracted my attention. I ran hastily back, and you may imagine my distress, when I found the beautiful pheasant lying lifeless upon the ground. It never breathed or showed the faintest sign of life afterward.

You may laugh at me, if you please, but I firmly believe that it died of home-sickness. What wonder that the free, beautiful, happy creature of God, torn from the sight of the broad, blue sky, the smiling river and the fresh, fragrant fir trees of its mountain home, and shut up in a dark, gloomy cabin, should have broken in twain its haughty, little heart? Yes, you may laugh, call me sentimental, etc., but I shall never forgive myself, for having killed, by inches, in my selfish and cruel kindness, that pretty creature.

Many people here call this bird a grouse; and those who have crossed the plains say that it is very much like a prairie hen. The Spanish name is *gallina del campo*, literally, "hen of the field." Since the death of my poor, little victim, I have been told that it is utterly impossible to tame one of these birds; and it is said, that if you put their eggs under a domestic fowl, the young, almost as soon as hatched, will instinctively run away to the beloved solitudes of their congenial homes; so passionately beats for liberty, each pulse of their free and wild natures.

Among the noteworthy events which have occurred since my last, I don't know how I came to forget, until the close of my letter, two smart shocks of an earthquake, to which we were treated a week ago. They were awe-inspiring, but after all were nothing in comparison to the timber-quake, an account of which I have given you above. But as F. is about to leave for the top of the Butte Mountains with a party of Rich Barians, and as I have much to do to prepare him for the journey, I must close.

LETTER ELEVENTH

A TRIP INTO THE MINES

From our Log Cabin, Indian Bar,
December 15, 1851

I LITTLE thought, dear M., that here, with the "green watching hills" as witnesses, amid a solitude so grand and lofty that it seems as if the faintest whisper of passion must be hushed by its holy stillness, I should have to relate the perpetration of one of those fearful deeds, which, were it for no other peculiarity than its startling suddenness—so utterly at variance with all *civilized* law—must make our beautiful California appear to strangers rather as a hideous phantom, than the flower-wreathed reality which she is.

Whether the life, which a few men, in the impertinent intoxication of power, have dared to crush out, was worth that of a fly, I do not know,—perhaps not; though God alone, methinks, can judge of the value of the soul upon which he has breathed. But certainly the effect upon the hearts of those who played the principal parts in the revolting scene referred to—a tragedy, in my simple judgment, so utterly useless—must be demoralizing in the extreme.

The facts in this sad case are as follows: Last fall, two men were arrested by their partners, on suspicion of having stolen from them eighteen hundred dollars in gold dust. The evidence was not sufficient to convict them, and they were acquitted. They were tried before a meeting of the miners—as at that time the law did not even *pretend* to wave its scepter over the place.

The prosecutors still believed them guilty, and fancied that the gold was hidden in a "coyote hole," near the camp from which it had been taken. They therefore watched the place narrowly while the suspected men remained on the Bar. They made no discoveries, however; and soon after the trial, the acquitted persons left the mountains for Marysville.

A few weeks ago, one of these men returned, and has spent most of the time since his arrival in loafing about the different bar-rooms upon the river. He is said to have been constantly intoxicated. As soon as the losers of the gold heard of his return, they bethought themselves of the "coyote hole," and placed about its entrance some brushwood and stones, in such a manner that no one could go into it without disturbing the arrangement of them. In the meanwhile the thief settled at Rich Bar, and pretended that he was in search of some gravel ground for mining purposes.

A few mornings ago, he returned to his boarding place —which he had left some hour earlier—with a spade in his hand, and as he laid it down, carelessly observed that he had "been out prospecting." The losers of the gold went, immediately after breakfast, as they had been in the habit of doing, to see if all was right at the "coyote hole." On this fatal day, they saw that the entrance had been disturbed, and going in, they found upon the ground, a money belt which had apparently just been cut open. Armed with this evidence of guilt, they confronted the suspected person and sternly accused him of having the gold in his possession. Singularly enough, he did not attempt a denial, but said that if they would not bring him to a trial, (which of course they promised) he would give it up immediately. He then informed them that they would

find it beneath the blankets of his *bunk*,—as those queer
shelves on which miners sleep, ranged one above another,
somewhat like the berths of the ship, are generally called.
There, sure enough, were six hundred dollars of the missing money, and the unfortunate wretch declared that his
partner had taken the remainder to the States.

By this time the excitingnews had spread all over the
Bar. A meeting of the miners was immediately convened,
the unhappy man taken into custody, a jury chosen, and a
judge, lawyer, etc., appointed. Whether the men, who had
just regained a portion of their missing property, made
any objections to the proceedings which followed, I know
not; if they had done so, however, it would have made no
difference, as the *people* had taken the matter entirely out
of their hands.

At one o'clock, so rapidly was the trial conducted, the
judge charged the jury, and gently insinuated that they
could do no less than to bring in with their verdict of
guilty, a sentence of *death*! Perhaps you know that when a
trial is conducted without the majesty of the law, the jury
are compelled to decide, not only upon the guilt of the
prisoner, but the mode of his punishment also. After a few
minutes' absence, the twelve men who had consented to
burden their souls with a responsibility so fearful, returned, and the foreman handed to the judge a paper,
from which he read the will of the *people*, as follows:
"That William Brown, convicted of stealing, etc., should,
in *one hour* from that time, be hung by the neck until he
was dead."

By the persuasions of some men more mildly disposed,
they granted him a respite of *three hours*, to prepare for
his sudden entrance into eternity. He employed the time
in writing in his native language (he is a Swede) to some

friends in Stockholm; God help them when that fatal post shall arrive; for no doubt *he*, also, although a criminal, was fondly garnered in many a loving heart.

He had exhibited during the trial, the utmost reckless-ness and *nonchalance*, had drank many times in the course of the day, and when the rope was placed about his neck, was evidently much intoxicated. All at once, however, he seemed startled into a consciousness of the awful reality of his position, and requested a few moments for prayer.

The execution was conducted by the jury, and was per-formed by throwing the cord, one end of which was at-tached to the neck of the prisoner, across the limb of a tree standing outside of the Rich Bar grave-yard; when all, who felt disposed to engage in so revolting a task, lifted the poor wretch from the ground, in the most awkward manner possible. The whole affair, indeed, was a piece of cruel butchery, though *that* was not intentional, but arose from the ignorance of those who made the preparations. In truth, life was only crushed out of him, by hauling the writhing body up and down several times in succession, by the rope which was wound round a large bough of his green-leafed gallows. Almost everybody was surprised at the severity of the sentence; and many, with their hands on the cord, did not believe even *then*, that it would be carried into effect, but thought that at the last moment, the jury would release the prisoner and substitute a milder punishment.

It is said that the crowd generally, seemed to feel the solemnity of the occasion; but many of the drunkards, who form a large part of the community on these Bars, laughed and shouted, as if it were a spectacle got up for their particular amusement. A disgusting specimen of in-toxicated humanity, struck with one of those luminous ideas peculiar to his class, staggered up to the victim, who was praying at the moment, and crowding a dirty rag into his almost unconscious hand, in a voice broken by a drunken hiccough, tearfully implored him to take his "handercher," and if he were *innocent*, (the man had not denied his guilt since first accused), to drop it as soon as he was drawn up into the air, but if *guilty*, not to let it fall on any account.

The body of the criminal was allowed to hang for some hours after the execution. It had commenced storming in the earlier part of the evening; and when those, whose business it was to inter the remains, arrived at the spot, they found them enwrapped in a soft, white shroud of feathery snow-flakes, as if pitying Nature had tried to hide from the offended face of heaven, the cruel deed which her mountain children had committed.

I have heard no one approve of this affair. It seems to have been carried on entirely by the more reckless part of the community. There is no doubt, however, that they seriously *thought* they were doing right, for many of them are kind and sensible men. They firmly believed that such an example was absolutely necessary for the protection of this community. Probably the recent case of "Little John," rendered this last sentence more severe than it otherwise would have been. The "Squire," of course, could do nothing (as in criminal cases the *people* utterly refuse to acknowledge his authority) but protest against the whole of the proceedings, which he did, in the usual legal manner.

If William Brown had committed a murder, or had even attacked a man for his money,—if he had been a quarrelsome, fighting character, endangering lives in his excitement, it would have been a very different affair. But with the exception of the crime for which he perished, (he *said* it was his first, and there is no reason to doubt the truth of his assertion), he was a harmless, quiet, inoffensive person.

You must not confound this miner's judgment with the doings of the noble *Vigilance Committee* of San Francisco. They are almost totally different in their organization and manner of proceeding. The Vigilance Committee had become absolutely necessary for the protection of society. It was composed of the best and wisest men in the city. They used their powers with a moderation unexampled in history, and they laid it down with a calm and quiet readiness which was absolutely sublime, when they found that legal justice had again resumed that course of stern, unflinching duty which should always be its characteristic. They took ample time for a thorough investigation of all the circumstances relating to the criminals who fell into their hands; and in *no* case have they hung a man, who had not been proved beyond the shadow of a doubt, to have committed at least *one* robbery in which life had been endangered, if not absolutely taken.

But by this time, dear M., you must be tired of the melancholy subject; and yet if I keep my promise of relating to you all that interests *us* in our new and strange life, I shall have to finish my letter with a catastrophe, in many respects more sad than that which I have just recounted.

At the commencement of our first storm, a hard working, industrious laborer, who had accumulated about eight hundred dollars, concluded to return to the States. As the snow had been falling but a few hours, when he, with two acquaintances, started from Rich Bar, no one doubted that they would not reach Marysville in perfect safety. They went on foot themselves, taking with them one mule to carry their blankets. For some unexplained reason, they took an unfrequented route. When the ex-

press man came in, he said that he met the two companions of R. eight miles beyond Buck's Rancho, which is the
first house one finds after leaving Rich Bar, and is only
fourteen miles distant from here.

These men had camped at an uninhabited cabin called
the "Frenchman's," where they had built a fire, and were
making themselves both merry and comfortable. They informed the express man, that they had left their *friend* (?)
three miles back, in a dying state. That the cold had been
too much for him, and that no doubt he was already dead.
They had brought away the money, and even the *blankets*
of the expiring wretch! They said that if they had stopped
with him, they would have been frozen themselves. But
even if their story is true, they must be the most brutal of
creatures, not to have made him as comfortable as possible, with *all* the blankets, and after they had built their
fire and got warm, to have returned and ascertained if he
were really dead.

On hearing the express man's report, several men who
had been acquainted with the deceased, started out to try
and discover his remains. They found his violin, broken
into several pieces, but all traces of the poor fellow himself had disappeared, probably forever.

In the meanwhile, some travelers had carried the same
news to Burke's Rancho, when several of the residents of
that place, followed the two men and overtook them to
Bidwell's Bar, where they had them arrested on suspicion
of murder. They protested their innocence, of course, and
one of them said that he would lead a party to the spot
where they had left the dying man. On arriving in the vicinity of the place, he at first stated that it was under one
tree, then another, and another, and at last ended by declaring that it was utterly impossible for him to remember
where they were camped at the time of R.'s death.

In this state of things nothing was to be done but to return to B.'s. When the excitement having somewhat subsided, they were allowed to proceed on their journey, the money—which they both swore R. had willed in his dying moments, to a near relation of one of these very men,—having been taken from them in order to be sent by express to the friends of the deceased in the States.

Although they have been acquitted, many shake their heads doubtfully at the whole transaction. It seems very improbable, that a man, accustomed all his life to hard labor and exposure, even although slightly unwell, as it is said he was, at the time, should have sunk under the cold during a walk of less than twenty miles, amid a gentle fall of snow and rain, when, as it is well known, the air is comparatively mild. It is to be hoped, however, that the companions of R. were brutal rather than criminal; though the desertion of a dying friend under such circumstances, even to the last unfeeling and selfish act, of removing from the expiring creature his blankets, is in truth almost as bad as actual murder.

I hope in my next, that I shall have something more cheerful than the above chapter of horrors, to relate. In the meanwhile, *adios*, and think as kindly as you can of the dear California, even though her lustrous skies gaze upon such barbarous deeds.

LETTER TWELFTH

RESIDENCE IN THE MINES

From our Log Cabin, Indian Bar,
January 27, 1852

I WISH that it were possible, dear M., to give you an idea of the perfect Saturnalia, which has been held upon the river for the last three weeks, without at the same time causing you to think *too* severely of our good Mountains. In truth, it requires not only a large intellect, but a large heart, to judge with becoming charity of the peculiar temptations of riches. A more generous, hospitable, intelligent and industrious people, than the inhabitants of the half-dozen Bars—of which Rich Bar is the nucleus—never existed; for you know how proverbially wearing it is to the nerves of manhood, to be entirely without either occupation or amusement; and that has been pre-eminently the case during the present month.

Imagine a company of enterprising and excitable young men, settled upon a sandy level, about as large as a poor widow's potato patch, walled in by sky-kissing hills—absolutely *compelled* to remain, on account of the weather, which has vetoed indefinitely their Exodus—with no place to ride or drive, even if they had the necessary vehicles and quadrupeds,—with no newspapers nor politics to interest them,—deprived of all books but a few dog-eared novels of

the poorest class,—churches, lectures, lyceums, theaters
and (most unkindest cut of all!) pretty girls, having become to these unhappy men mere myths,—without *one* of
the thousand ways of passing time peculiar to civilization,—most of them living in damp, gloomy cabins, where
Heaven's dear light can enter only by the door,—and,
when you add to all these disagreeables the fact that, during the never-to-be-forgotten month, the most remorseless, persevering rain which ever set itself to work to drive
humanity mad, has been pouring doggedly down, sweeping away bridges, lying in uncomfortable puddles about
nearly all the habitations, wickedly insinuating itself beneath un-umbrella-protected shirt-collars, generously
treating to a shower-bath *and* the rheumatism sleeping bipeds, who did not happen to have an India-rubber blanket,—and, to crown all, rendering mining utterly impossible,—you cannot wonder that even the most moral
should have become somewhat reckless.

The Saturnalia commenced on Christmas evening, at
the Humboldt, which on that very day, had passed into
the hands of new proprietors. The most gorgeous preparations were made for celebrating the *two* events. The bar
was re-trimmed with red calico, the bowling alley had a
new lining of the coarsest and whitest cotton cloth, and
the broken lamp-shades were replaced by whole ones. All
day long, patient mules could be seen descending the hill,
bending beneath casks of brandy and baskets of champagne, and, for the first time in the history of that celebrated building, the floor (wonderful to relate, it *has* a
floor,) was *washed*, at a lavish expenditure of some fifty
pails of water, the using up of one entire broom, and the
melting away of sundry bars of the best yellow soap; after
which, I am told that the enterprising and benevolent individuals, who had undertaken the Herculean task, suc-

ceeded in washing the boards through the hopeless load of
dirt, which had accumulated upon them during the summer and autumn. All these interesting particulars were
communicated to me by "Ned," when he brought up dinner. That distinguished individual himself was in his element, and in a most intense state of perspiration and excitement at the same time.

About dark, we were startled by the loudest hurras,
which arose at the sight of an army of India-rubber coats,
(the rain was falling in riversful,) each one enshrouding a
Rich Barian, which was rapidly descending the hill. This
troop was headed by the "General," who—lucky man that
he is—waved on high, instead of a banner, a *live* lantern,
actually composed of tin and window-glass, and evidently
intended by its maker to act in no capacity but that *of* a
lantern! The "General" is the largest and tallest and—with
one exception, I think—the oldest man upon the river. He
is about fifty, I should fancy, and wears a snow-white
beard of such immense dimensions, in both length and
thickness, that any elderly Turk would expire with envy,
at the mere sight of it. Don't imagine the *he* is a reveler; by
no means; the gay crowd followed *him*, for the same reason that the king followed Madame Blaize, "because he
went before."

At nine o'clock in the evening, they had an oyster and
champagne supper in the Humboldt, which was very gay
with toasts, songs, speeches, etc. I believe that the company danced all night; at any rate, they were dancing
when I went to sleep, and they were dancing when I woke
the next morning. The revel was kept up in this mad way
for three days, growing wilder every hour. Some never
slept at all during that time. On the fourth day, they got
past dancing, and, lying in drunken heaps about the bar-
room, commenced a most unearthly howling;—some

barked like dogs, some roared like bulls, and others hissed like serpents and geese. Many were too far gone to imitate anything but their own animalized selves. The scene, from the description I have had of it, must have been a complete illustration of the fable of Circe and her fearful transformations. Some of these bacchanals were among the most respectable and respected men upon the river. Many of them had resided here for more than a year, and had never been seen intoxicated before. It seemed as if they were seized with a reckless mania for pouring down liquor, which, as I said above, everything conspired to foster and increase.

Of course, there were some who kept themselves aloof from these excesses; but they were few, and were not allowed to enjoy their sobriety in peace. The revelers formed themselves into a mock vigilance committee, and when one of these unfortunates appeared outside, a constable, followed by those who were able to keep their legs, brought him before the Court, where he was tried on some amusing charge, and *invariably* sentenced to "treat the crowd." The prisoners had generally the good sense to submit cheerfully to their fate.

Towards the latter part of the week, people where compelled to be a little more quiet from sheer exhaustion; but on New Year's day, when there was a grand dinner at Rich Bar, the excitement broke out, if possible, worse than ever. The same scenes in a more or less aggravated form, in proportion as the strength of the actors held out, were repeated at Smith's Bar and "The Junction."

Nearly every day, I was dreadfully frightened, by seeing a boat-load of intoxicated men fall into the river, where nothing but the fact of their *being* intoxicated, saved many of them from drowning. One morning, about thirty dollars worth of bread, (it must have been "tipsy cake,")

which the baker was conveying to Smith's Bar, fell over-
board, and sailed merrily away towards Marysville. People
passed the river in a boat, which was managed by a pulley
and a rope, that was strained across it from Indian Bar to
the opposite shore.

Of the many acquaintances, who had been in the habit
of calling nearly every evening three, only, appeared in the
cabin during as many weeks. Now, however, the Saturnalia is about over. "Ned" and "Choch," have nearly fid-
dled themselves into their respective graves,—the claret (a
favorite wine with miners,) and oysters are exhausted,—
brandied fruits are rarely seen, and even port wine is beginning to look scarce. Old callers occasionally drop in,
looking dreadfully sheepish and subdued, and *so* sorry,—
and people are evidently arousing themselves from the
bacchanal madness, into which they were so suddenly and
so strangely drawn.

With the exception of my last, this is the most unpleas-
ant letter which I have ever felt it my duty to write to you.
Perhaps you will wonder that I should touch upon such a
disagreeable subject at all. But I am bound, Molly, by my
promise, to give you a *true* picture (as much as in me lies,)
of mining life and its peculiar temptations, "nothing ex-
tenuating nor setting down aught in malice." But with all
their failings, believe me, the miners, as a class, possess
many truly admirable characteristics.

I have had rather a stupid time during the storm. We
had been in the habit of taking frequent rows upon the
river in a funny little toppling canoe, carved out of a log.
The bridge at one end of our boating ground and the
rapids at the other, made quite a pretty lake. To be sure it
was so small that we generally passed and repassed its
beautiful surface at least thirty times in an hour. But we
did not mind *that*, I can assure you. We were only *too* glad

to be able to go onto the water at all. I used to return,
loaded down with the magnificent large leaves of some
aquatic plant, which the gentle frosts had painted with the
most gorgeous colors, lots of fragrant mint, and a few
wan, white flowers, which had lingered past their autumnal glory. The richest hot-house bouquet could never give
me half the pleasure, which I took in arranging in a pretty
vase of purple and white, those gorgeous leaves. They
made me think of Moorish Arabesques; so quaint and
bizarre, and at the same time dazzlingly brilliant were the
varied tints. They were in their glory at evening; for like an
oriental beauty, they *lighted up* splendidly. Alas! where
one little month ago, my pretty lake lay laughing up at the
stars, a turbid torrent rushes noisily by;—the poor little
canoe was swept away with the bridge, and splendid leaves
hide their bright heads forever beneath the dark waters.

But I am not entirely bereft of the beautiful. From my
last walk, I brought home a tiny bit of *out-doors*, which
through all the long, rainy months that are to come, will
sing to me silently, yet eloquently, of the blue and gold of
the vanished summer, and the crimson and purple of its
autumn. It is a branch, gathered from that prettiest feature of mountain scenery, a moss-grown fir-tree. You will
see them at every step, standing all lovely in this graceful
robe. It is in color, a vivid pea-green, with little hard
flowers, which look more like dots than anything else, and
contrast beautifully with the deeper verdure of the fir.
The branch, which I brought home, I have placed above
my window. It is three feet in length and as large round as
a person's arm; and there it remains, a cornice wreathed
with purple-starred tapestry, whose wondrous beauty no
upholsterer can ever match.

I have got the prettiest New Year's present. You will
never guess what it is, so I shall have to tell you. On the eve

of the year, as the "General" was lifting a glass of water, which had just been brought from the river, to his lips, he was startled at the sight of a tiny fish. He immediately put it into a glass jar and gave it to me. It is that most lovely of all the creatures of Thetis, a spotted trout, a little more than two inches in length. Its back of mingled green and gold, is splashed with dots of the richest sable. A mark of a dark ruby color, in shape like an anchor, crowns its elegant little head. Nothing can be prettier than the delicate wings of pale purple, with which its snowy belly is faintly penciled. Its jet black eyes, rimmed with silver, within a circlet of rare sea-blue, gleam like diamonds, and its whole graceful shape is gilded with a shimmering sheen, infinitely lovely. When I watch it from across the room, as it glides slowly round its crystal palace, it reminds me of a beam of many-colored light; but when it glides up and down in its gay playfulness, it gleams through the liquid atmosphere like a box of shining silver. "A thing of beauty is a joy forever;" and, truly, I never weary watching the perfected loveliness of my graceful little captive.

In the list of my deprivations, above written, I forgot to mention a fact, which I know will gain me the sympathy of all carniverously disposed people. It is, that we have had no *fresh meat* for nearly a month! Dark and ominous rumors are also floating through the moist air, to the effect that the potatoes and onions are about to give out! But don't be alarmed, dear Molly. There is no danger of a famine. For have we not got wagon loads of hard, dark hams, whose indurated hearts nothing but the sharpest knife and the stoutest arm can penetrate? Have we not got quintals of dreadful mackerel, fearfully crystalized in black salt? Have we not barrels upon barrels of rusty pork; and flour enough to victual a large army for the next two years? Yea, verily, have we; and more also. For we have oysters in cans, preserved meats and sardines, (*apropos*, I *detest* them) by the hundred box full.

So hush the trembling of that tender little heart and shut those tearful and alarmed eyes, while I press a good-night kiss on their drooping lids.

LETTER THIRTEENTH

RESIDENCE IN THE MINES

From our Log Cabin, Indian Bar,
February 27, 1852

YOU WILL find this missive, dear M., a journal, rather than a letter; for the few insignificant events, which have taken place since I last wrote to you, will require but three lines apiece for their recital. But stop; when I say insignificant, I forget one all-important misfortune, which, for our sins I suppose, has befallen us, in the sudden departure of our sable Paganini.

> Yes; Vattal Ned to the valley hath gone,
>   In a Marysville kitchen you'll find him;
> Two rusty pistols he girded on,
>   And his violin hung behind him.

His fiddle is heard no more on all the Bar, and silence reigns through the calico halls of the Humboldt. His bland smile and his dainty plats, his inimitably choice language and his pet tambourine, his woolly corkscrew and his really beautiful music, have I fear vanished forever from the mountains.

Just before he left, he found a birth-day, which belonged to himself; and was observed all the morning thereof, standing about in spots, a perfect picture of perplexity painted in burnt umber. Inquiry being made by sympathizing friends as to the cause of his distress, he answered, "that having no fresh meat, he could not prepare a dinner for the log-cabin, worthy of the occasion!"

But no circumstance can put a man of genius entirely *hors du combat*. Confine him in a dungeon, banish him to an uninhabited island, place him solitary and alone in a boundless desert, deprive him of all but life, and he will still achieve wonders. With the iron hams, the piscatory phenomena referred to in my last, and a can of really excellent oysters, Ned's birth-day dinner was a *chef d'oeuvre*. He accompanied it with a present of a bottle of very good Champagne, requesting us to drink it (which we *did*, not having the fear of temperance societies, or Maine law liquor bills before our eyes,) in honor of his having dropped another year into the returnless past.

There has been a great excitement here, on account of the fancied discovery of valuable quartz mines, in the vicinity of the American Rancho, which is situated about twenty miles from this place. Half the people upon the river went out there, for the purpose of "prospecting" and "staking claims." The quartz apparently paid admirably; several companies were speedily formed, and men sent to Hamilton, the county seat, to record the various claims. F. himself went out there, and remained several days. Now, however, the whole excitement has turned out to be a complete humbug. The quicksilver which was procured at the Rancho, for the testing of the quartz, the victims declare was "salted," and they accuse the *Rancheros* of conniving at the fraud, for the purpose of making money out of those who were compelled to lodge and board with them while "prospecting." The accused affirm, that if there was any deception (which, however, is beyond the shadow of a doubt) they, also, were deceived; and as they appear like honest men enough, I am inclined to believe them.

Just now, there is a new quartz mine excitement. A man has engaged to lead a company to the golden and crystallized spot. Probably this, also, will prove like the other, a mere yellow buble. But even if as rich as he says, it will be of little value at present, on account of the want of suitable machinery; that, now in use, being so expensive, and wasting so much of the precious metal, that it leaves the miner but little profit. It is thought, however, by men of judgment, that in a few years, when the proper way of working them to advantage has been discovered, the quartz mines will be more profitable than any others in California.

A few days ago, we had another specimen of illegal, but in this case, at least, extremely equitable justice. Five men left the river without paying their debts. A meeting of the miners was convened, and "Yank," who possesses an iron frame, the perseverance of a bulldog, and a constitution which never knew fatigue, was appointed, with another person, to go in search of the culprits, and bring them back to Indian Bar. He found them a few miles from this place, and returned with them in triumph and alone—his friend having been compelled to remain behind, on account of excessive fatigue. The self-constituted court, after a fair trial, obliged the five men to settle all liabilities before they again left the river.

Last week, the Frenchmen on the river celebrated the revolution of Feb. 1848. What kind of a time they had during the day I know not; but in the evening (*apropos*, part of them reside at Missouri Bar) they formed a torch-light procession, and marched to Rich Bar, which, by the way, takes airs upon itself, and considers itself as a *Town*. They made quite a picturesque appearance as they wound up the hill, each one carrying a tiny pine tree, the top of which was encircled with a diadem of flame, beautifully lighting up the darker verdure beneath, and gleaming like a spectral crown through the moonless, misty evening. We could not help laughing at their watchwords. They ran in this wise; "Shorge Washingtone, James K. Polk, Napoleon Bonaparte! Liberte, Egalite, Fraternite! Andrew Jacksone, President Filmore and Lafayette!" I give them to you, word for word, as I took them down at the time.

Since the bridges have been swept away, I have been to Rich Bar but once. It is necessary to go over the hill now, and the walk is a very wearisome one. It is much more pleasant to live on the hills, than on the Bar, and during our walk we passed two or three cosy little cabins, nestling in broad patches of sunlight, and surrounded with ample space for a promenade, which made me quite envious. Unfortunately, F.'s profession renders it desirable that he should reside where the largest number of people congregate, and then the ascent to the habitable portion of the hill is as steep as any part of that leading into Rich Bar, and it would be impossible for him to walk up and down it several times a day, a task which he would be compelled to perform if we resided there. For that reason I make myself as happy as possible where I am.

I have been invited to dine at the best built log cabin on the river. It is situated on the hill of which I have just been writing, and is owned by five or six intelligent, hard-working, sturdy young men. Of course, it has no floor, but it boasts a perfect marvel of a fireplace. They never pretend to split the wood for it, but merely fall a giant fir tree, strip it of its branches, and cut it into pieces the length of the aforesaid wonder. This cabin is lighted in a manner truly ingenious. Three feet in length of a log on one side of the room is removed and glass jars inserted in its place; the space around the necks of said jars being filled with clay. This novel idea is really an excellent substitute for window glass. You will, perhaps, wonder where they procure enough of the material for such a purpose.

They are brought here in enormous quantities containing brandied fruits; for there is no possible luxury connected with drinking, which is procurable in California, that cannot be found in the mines; and the very men, who fancy it a piece of wicked extravagance to *buy* bread, because they can save a few dimes by *making* it themselves, are often those who think nothing of spending from fifteen to twenty dollars a night in the bar-rooms. There is at this moment, a perfect Pelion upon Ossa-like pile of beautiful glass jars, porter, ale, Champagne and claret bottles lying in front of my window. The latter are a very convenient article for the manufacture of the most enchantingly primitive lanterns. Any one in want of a utensil of this kind has but to step to his cabin door, take up a claret or Champagne bottle, knock off the bottom, and dropping into the neck thereof, through the opening thus made, a candle, to have a most excellent lantern. And the beauty of it is, that every time you wish to use such a thing, you can have a *new* one.

But to return to my description of the cabin. It consists of one very large room, in the back part of which are neatly stored several hundred sacks of flour, a large quantity of potatoes, sundry kegs of butter, and plenty of hams and mackerel. The furniture consists of substantial wooden stools, and in these I observed that our friends followed the fashion—no two of them being made alike. Some stood proudly forth in all the grandeur of four legs, others affected the classic grace of the ancient tripod, while a few, shrank bashfully into corners on one stubbed stump. Some round, some square, and some triangular in form; several were so high that when enthroned upon them, the ends of my toes just touched the ground, and others were so low, that on rising I carried away a large portion of the soil upon my unfortunate skirts. Their bunks, as they call them, were arranged in two rows along one side of the cabin, each neatly covered with a dark blue or red blanket. A handsome oil cloth was spread upon the table, and the service consisted of tin plates, a pretty set of stone China cups and saucers, and some good knives and forks, which looked almost as bright as if they had just come from the cutlers. For dinner, we had boiled beef and ham, broiled mackerel, potatoes, splendid new bread, made by one of the gentlemen of the house, coffee, milk, (Mr. B. has bought a cow, and now and then we get a wee-drop of milk,) and the most delicious Indian meal parched that I ever tasted. I have been very particular in describing this cabin, for it is the best built, and by far the best ap-pointed one upon the river.

I have said nothing about candlesticks as yet, I must confess that in *them*, the spice of life is carried almost too far. One gets satiated with their wonderful variety. I will mention but two or three of these make-shifts. Bottles, *without* the bottoms knocked off, are general favorites. Many however, exhibit an insane admiration for match boxes, which, considering that they *will* keep falling *all* the time, and leaving the entire house in darkness, and scattering spermaceti in every direction, is rather an in-convenient taste. Some fancy blocks of wood, with an ornamental balustrade of three nails, and I *have* seen praiseworthy candles making desperate efforts to stand straight in tumblers! Many of our friends, with a beautiful and sublime faith in spermaceti and good luck, eschew everything of the kind, and you will often find their tables picturesquely covered with splashes of the former article, elegantly ornamented with little strips of black wick.

The sad forbodings mentioned in a former letter have come to pass. For some weeks, with the exceptions of two or three families, every one upon the river has been out of

butter, onions and potatoes. Our kind friends upon the
hill, who have a little remaining, sent me a few pounds of
the former the other day. Ham, mackerel and bread, with
occasionally a treat of the precious butter, has been literally our only food for a long time. The Rancheros have
not driven in any beef for several weeks; and although it is
so pleasant on the Bars, the cold on the mountains still
continues so intense that the trail remained impassable to
mules.

The weather here, for the past five weeks, has been like
the Indian summer at home. Nearly every day I take a
walk up on to the hill back of our cabin; nobody lives
there, it is so very steep. I have a cosy little seat in the
fragrant bosom of some evergreen shrubs where often I
remain for hours. It is almost like death to mount to my
favorite spot, the path is so steep and stony, but it is new
life when I arrive there, to sit in the shadow of the pines,
and listen to the plaintive wail of the wind as it surges
through their musical leaves, and to gaze down upon the
tented Bar lying in somber gloom,—for as yet the sun does
not shine upon it,—and the foam-flaked river, and around
at the awful mountain, splashed here and there with broad
patches of snow, or reverently upward into the stainless
blue of our unmatchable sky.

This letter is much longer than I thought it would be
when I commenced it, and I believe that I have been as
minutely particular as ever you can desire. I have mentioned everything that has happened since I last wrote. O!
I was very near forgetting a present of two ring doves,
(alas! they had been shot) and a blue jay which I received
yesterday. We had them roasted for dinner last evening.
The former were very beautiful, approaching in hue more
nearly to a French gray, than what is generally called a
dun color, with a perfect ring of ivory encircling each

pretty neck. The blue jay was exactly like its namesake in the States.

Good-bye, my dear M., and remember, that the *same* sky, though not quite so beautiful a portion of it, which smiles upon *me* in sunny California, bends lovingly over *you* in cold, dreary, but in spite of its harsh airs, beloved New England.

LETTER FOURTEENTH

RESIDENCE IN THE MINES

From our Log Cabin, Indian Bar,
March 15, 1852

THIS FIFTEENTH day of March, has risen upon us with all the primeval splendor of the birth-morn of creation. The lovely river—having resumed its crimson border, (the so-long idle miners being again busily at work,) glides by, laughing gaily, leaping and clapping its glad waves joyfully in the golden sunlight. The feathery fringe of the fir-trees glitters, like emerald, in the luster bathing air. A hundred tiny rivulets flash down from the brow of the mountains, as if some mighty Titan, standing on the other side, had flung athwart their greenness, a chaplet of radiant pearls. Of the large quantities of snow which have fallen within the past fortnight, a few patches of shining whiteness, high up among the hills, alone remain; while, to finish the picture, the lustrous heaven of California, looking "further off" than ever, through the wonderfully transparent atmosphere, and for that very reason, infinitely more beautiful, bends over all the matchless blue of its resplendent arch. Ah! the heaven of the Golden Land. To you, living beneath the murky skies of New England, how unimaginably lovely it is! A small poetess has said that "*She* could not love a scene, where the blue sky was *always* blue." I think that it is not so with me; I am sure that I never weary of the succession of rainless months, and the azure dome, day after day so mistless, which bends above this favored country.

Between each stroke of the pen, I stop to glance at that splendor, whose sameness never fails; but now, a flock of ringdoves break for a moment, with dots of purple, its monotonous beauty; and the carol of a tiny bird, (the first of the season,) though I cannot see the darling, fills the joyful air with its mating song.

All along the side of the hill, rising behind the Bar, and on the latter also, glance spots of azure and crimson, in the forms of blue and red-shirted miners, bending steadily over pick-axe and shovel; reminding one involuntarily of the muck-gatherer in "Pilgrim's Progress." But, no, that is an unjust association of ideas; for many of these men are toiling thus wearily for laughing-lipped children, calm-browed wives, or saintly mothers, gathering around the household hearth, in some far-away country. Even among the few now remaining on the river, there are wanderers from the whole broad earth; and, O! what a world of poetic recollection is suggested by their living presence! From happiest homes, and such luxuriant lands, has the golden magnet drawn its victims. From those palm-girdled isles of the Pacific, which Melville's gifted pen has consecrated to such beautiful romance; from Indies, blazing through the dim past with funeral pyres, upon whose perfumed flame, ascended to God, the chaste souls of her devoted wives; from the grand old woods of classic Greece, haunted by nymph and satyr, naiad and grace, grape-crowned Bacchus and beauty-zoned Venus; from the polished heart of artificial Europe, from the breezy backwoods of young America, from the tropical languor of Asian Savannah; from *every* spot shining through the rosy

light of beloved old fables, or consecrated by lofty deeds
of heroism or devotion, or shrined in our heart of hearts,
as the sacred home of some great or gifted one, they
gather to the golden harvest.

You will hear in the same day, almost at the same time,
the lofty melody of the Spanish language, the piquant
polish of the French, (which, though not a *musical*
tongue, is the most *useful* of them all,) the silver, changing
clearness of the Italian, the harsh gangle of the German,
the hissing precision of the English, the liquid sweetness
of the Kanaka, and the sleep-inspiring languor of the East
Indian. To complete the catalogue, there is the *native* Indian, with his guttural vocabulary of twenty words! When
I hear these sounds so strangely different, and look at the
speakers, I fancy them a living polyglot of the languages, a
perambulating picture gallery, illustrative of national variety in form and feature.

By the way, speaking of languages, nothing is more
amusing, than to observe the different styles, in which the
generality of the Americans talk *at* the unfortunate Spaniard. In the first place, many of them really believe, that
when they have learned *sabe* and *vamos*, (two words
which they seldom use in the right place,) *poco tiempo, si,*
and *bueno*, (the last they *will* persist in pronouncing
whayno,) they have the whole of the glorious Castilian at
their tongue's end. Some, however, eschew the above
words entirely, and innocently fancy, that by splitting the
tympanum of an unhappy foreigner, in screaming forth
their sentences in good solid English, they can be surely
understood; others, at the imminent risk of dislocating
their own limbs and the jaws of their listeners, by the
laughs which their efforts elicit, make the most excruciatingly grotesque gestures, and think that *that* is speaking
Spanish. The majority, however, place a most beautiful

and touching faith in *broken English*, and when they murder it, with the few words of Castilian quoted above, are firmly convinced, that it is nothing but their "ugly dispositions" which makes the Spaniards pretend not to understand them.

One of those dear, stupid Yankees, who *will*, now and then, venture out of sight of the smoke of their own chimneys, as far as California, was relating *his* experience in this particular the other day. It seems that he had lost a horse somewhere among the hills, and during his search for it, met a gentlemanly Chileno, who, with national suavity, made the most desperate efforts to understand the questions put to him. Of course, *Chileno* was so stupid that he did not succeed, for it is not possible that one of the "Great American People" could fail to express himself clearly, even in Hebrew, if he takes it into his cute head, to speak that ancient, but highly respectable, language. Our Yankee friend, however, would not allow the poor fellow even the excuse of stupidity, but declared that he only "played possum from sheer *ugliness*." "Why," he added, in relating the circumstance, "the cross, old rascal pretended not to understand his own language, though I said as plainly as possible, '*Señor, sabe mi horso vamos poco tempo?*' which, perhaps, you don't know," he proceeded to say, (in a benevolent desire to enlighten our ignorance and teach us a little Castilian,) "means, 'Sir, I have lost my horse, have you seen it?' " I am ashamed to acknowledge, that we did *not* know the above written Anglo-Spanish sentence to mean *that*! The honest fellow concluded his story by declaring, (and it is a common remark with uneducated Americans) with a most self-glorifying air of *pity* for the poor Spaniards, "They ain't kinder like *eour* folks,"—or, as the universal Aunt Somebody used so expressively to observe, "Somehow, they ain't *folksy!*"

The mistakes made on the other side, are often quite as amusing. Dr. Cañas related to us a laughable anecdote of a countryman of his, with whom he happened to camp, on his first arrival in San Francisco. None of the party could speak a word of English, and the person referred to, as ignorant as the rest, went out to purchase bread, which he procured, by laying down some money, and pointing to a loaf of that necessary edible. He probably heard a person use the words "some bread," for he rushed home, Cañas said, in a perfect burst of newly acquired wisdom and informed his friends that he had found out the English for *pan*, and that when they wished any of that article, they need but enter a bakeshop, and utter the word *sombrero*, in order to obtain it! His hearers were delighted to know *that* much of the *infernal lengua*, greatly marveling, however, that the same word which meant *hat*, in Castilian, should mean *bread* in English. The Spaniards have a saying, to the following effect, "Children speak in Italian, ladies speak in French, God speaks in Spanish, and the Devil speaks in English."

I commenced this letter with the intention of telling you about the weary, weary storm, which has not only thrown a damp over our spirits, but has saturated them, as it has everything else, with a deluge of moisture. The Storm King commenced his reign (or rain) on the twenty-eighth of February, and proved himself a perfect Proteus during his residence with us. For one entire week, he descended daily and nightly without an hour's cessation, in a forty Niagara power of water; and just as we were getting reconciled to this wet state of affairs, and were thinking seriously of learning to swim, one gloomy evening when we least expected such a change, he stole softly down, and garlanded us in a wreath of shining snow-flakes, and lo! the next morning you would have thought that some great white bird had shed its glittering feathers all over rock,

tree, hill and bar; he finished his vagaries by loosening, rat-
tling and crushing upon this devoted spot, a small skyful
of hailstones, which, aided by a terrific wind, waged terrible warfare against the frail tents, and the calico-shirt
huts, and made even the shingles on the roofs of the log-
cabins tremble amid their nails.

The river, usually so bland and smiling, looked really
terrific. It rose to an unexampled height, and tore along its
way, a perfect mass of dark-foamed, turbid waves. At one
time we had serious fears that the water would cover the
whole bar, for it approached within two or three feet of
the Humboldt. A sawmill, which had been built at a great
expense by two gentlemen of Rich Bar, in order to be
ready for the sawing of lumber, for the extensive fluming
operations which are in contemplation this season, was
entirely swept away,—nearly ruining, (it is said,) the
owner. I heard a great shout early one morning, and running to the window, had the sorrow to see wheels, planks,
etc., sailing merrily down the river. All along the banks of
the stream, men were trying to save the more valuable portions of the mill, but the torrent was so furious that it was
utterly impossible to rescue a plank. How the haughty
river seemed to laugh to scorn the feeble efforts of man!
How its mad waves tossed in wild derision, the costly
workmanship of his skilful hands! But know, proud Rio
de las Plumas, that these very men, whose futile efforts
you fancy that you have for once so gloriously defeated,
will gather from beneath your lowest depths the beautiful
ore, which you thought you had hidden forever and forever, beneath your azure beauty!

It is certainly most amusing, to hear of the different
plans which the poor miners invented to pass the time during the trying season of rains. Of course, poker and
euchre, whist and nine-pins, to say nothing of monte and
faro, are now in constant requisition. But as a person

would starve to death on *toujours des perdrix*, so a man cannot *always* be playing cards. Some *literary* bipeds, I have been told, reduced to the last degree of intellectual destitution, in a beautiful spirit of self-martyrdom, betook themselves to blue blankets, bunks and Ned Buntline's novels. And one day an unhappy youth went pen-mad, and in a melancholy fit of authorship wrote a thrilling account of our dreadful situation, which, directed to the editor of a Marysville paper, was sealed up in a keg and set adrift, and is at this moment, no doubt, stranded, high and dry, in the streets of Sacramento, for it is generally believed, that the cities of the plain have been under water during the storm. The chief amusement, however, has been the raffling of gold rings. There is a silversmith here, who, like the rest of the miserable inhabitants, having nothing to do, discovered that he could make gold rings. Of course every person must have a specimen of his workmanship, and the next thing was to raffle it off. The winner generally repeating the operation. Nothing was done or talked of for some days, but this important business.

I have one of these rings, which is really very beautifully finished, and, although, perhaps at home, it would look vulgar, there is a sort of massive and barbaric grandeur about it, which seems well-suited to our wild life of the hills. I shall send you one of these, which will be to you a curiosity, and will doubtless look strangely enough amid the graceful and airy politeness of French jewelry. But I think that it will be interesting to you, as having been manufactured in the mines, by an inexperienced workman, and without the necessary tools. If it is too hideous to be worn upon your slender little finger, you can have it engraved for a seal, and attach it as a charm to your watch chain.

Last evening, Mr. C. showed us a specimen ring which he had just finished. It is the handsomest *natural* specimen that I ever saw. Pure gold is generally dull in hue, but this is of a most beautiful shade of yellow, and extremely brilliant. It is, in shape and size, exactly like the flower of the jonquil. In the center, is inserted, with all the nice finish of art, (or rather of Nature, for it is her work) a polished piece of quartz, of the purest shade of pink; and between each radiant petal is set a tiny crystal of colorless quartz, every one of which flashes like a real diamond. It is known beyond doubt, to be a real live specimen, as many saw it when it was first taken from the earth, and the owner has carried it carelessly in his pocket for months. We would gladly have given fifty dollars for it, though its nominal value is only about an ounce, but it is already promised, as a present, to a gentleman in Marysville. Although rather a clumsy ring, it would make a most unique broach, and, indeed, is almost the *only* piece of unmanufactured ore, which I have ever seen, that I would be willing to wear. I have a piece of gold, which, without alteration, except, of course engraving, will make a beautiful seal. It is in the shape of an eagle's head, and is wonderfully perfect. It was picked up from the surface of the ground, by a gentleman, on his first arrival here, and he said that he would give it to the next lady to whom he should be introduced. He carried it in his purse for more than a year, when, in obedience to the promise made when he found it, it became the property of your humble servant, Shirley.

The other day a hole caved in, burying up to the neck two unfortunates, who were in it at the time. Luckily, they were but slightly injured.

T. is at present attending a man at the junction, who was stabbed very severely in the back during a drunken frolic. The people have not taken the slightest notice of this affair, although for some days the life of the wounded man was despaired of. The perpetrator of the deed had not the slightest provocation from his unfortunate victim.

LETTER FIFTEENTH

RESIDENCE IN THE MINES

From our Log Cabin, Indian Bar,
April 10, 1852

I HAVE been haunted all day, my dear M., with an intense ambition to write you a letter, which shall be dreadfully commonplace and severely utilitarian in its style and contents. Not but that my epistles are *always* commonplace enough, (spirits of Montague and Sevigne, forgive me!) but hitherto I have not really *tried* to make them so. Now, however, I *intend* to be stupidly prosy, with malice aforethought, and without one mitigating circumstance, except, perchance, it be the temptations of that abovementioned ambitious little devil to palliate my crime.

You would certainly wonder, were you seated where I now am, how any one with a quarter of a soul, *could* manufacture herself into a bore, amid such surroundings as these. The air is as balmy as that of a mid-summer's day in the sunniest valleys of New England. It is four o'clock in the evening, and I am sitting on a segar-box outside of our cabin. From this spot not a person is to be seen, except a man who is building a new wing to the "Humboldt." Not a human sound, but a slight noise made by the aforesaid individual, in tacking on a roof of blue drilling to the room which he is finishing, disturbs the stillness which fills this purest air. I confess that it is difficult to fix my eyes upon the dull paper, and my fingers upon the duller pen with which I am soiling it. Almost every other minute, I find myself stopping to listen to the ceaseless river-psalm, or to gaze up into the wondrous depths of the Cali-

fornia Heaven; to watch the graceful movements of the
pretty brown lizards, jerking up their impudent little
heads above a moss-wrought log which lies before me, or
to mark the dancing water-shadow on the canvas door of
the bake-shop opposite; to follow with childish eyes the
flight of a golden butterfly, curious to know if it will
crown, with a capital of winged beauty, that column of
Nature's carving, the pine stump rising at my feet, or
whether it will flutter down (for it is dallying coquettishly
around them both,) upon that slate-rock beyond, shining
so darkly lustrous through a flood of yellow sunlight; or I
lazily turn my head, wondering if I know the blue or red-
shirted miner who is descending the precipitous hill behind me. In sooth, Molly, it is easy to be commonplace at
all times, but I confess that, just at present, I find it difficult to be utilitary; the saucy lizards—the great, orange-
dotted butterflies—the still, solemn cedars—the sailing
smoke-wreath and the vaulted splendor above, are wooing
me so winningly to higher things.

But, as I said before, I have an ambition that way, and I
will succeed. You are such a good-natured little thing,
dear, that I know you will meekly allow yourself to be
victimized into reading the profound and prosy remarks
which I shall make, in my efforts to initiate you into the
mining polity of this place. Now you may rest assured that
I shall assert nothing upon the subject which is not perfectly correct; for have I not earned a character for in-
quisitiveness, (and you know that does *not* happen to be
one of my failings,) which I fear will cling to me through
life, by my persevering questions to all the unhappy
miners from whom I thought I could gain any information. Did I not martyrize myself into a human mule, by
descending to the bottom of a dreadful pit, (suffering
mortal terror all the time, least it should cave in upon me,)

actuated by a virtuous desire to see with my own two eyes
the process of underground mining, thus enabling myself
to be stupidly correct in all my statements thereupon?
Did I not ruin a pair of silk velvet slippers, lame my ankles
for a week, and draw a "browner horror" over my already
sun-burnt face, in a wearisome walk miles away, to the
head of the "ditch," as they call the prettiest little rivulet
(though the work of men)—that I ever saw; yea, verily,
this have I done for the express edification of yourself,
and the rest of your curious tribe, to be rewarded, probably, by the impertinent remark,—"What *does* that little
goose, 'Dame Shirley,' think that *I* care about such
things?" But madam, in spite of your sneer, I shall proceed in my allotted task.

In the first place, then, as to the discovery of gold. In
California, at least, it must be confessed, that in this particular, science appears to be completely at fault;—or, as an
intelligent and well-educated miner remarked to us the
other day, "I maintain that science is the blindest guide
that one could have on a gold-finding expedition. Those
men, who judge by the appearance of the soil, and depend
upon geological calculations, are invariably disappointed,
while the ignorant adventurer, who digs just for the sake
of digging, is almost sure to be successful." I suppose that
the above observation is quite correct, as all whom we
have questioned upon the subject repeat, in substance, the
same thing. Wherever Geology has said that gold *must* be,
there, perversely enough, it lies not; and wherever her
ladyship has declared that it could *not* be, there has it
oftenest garnered up in miraculous profusion the yellow
splendor of its virgin beauty. It is certainly very painful to
a well-regulated mind to see the irreverent contempt,
shown by this beautiful mineral, to the dictates of science;
but what better can one expect from the "root of all

evil?" As well as can be ascertained, the most lucky of the mining Columbuses have been ignorant sailors; and foreigners, I fancy, are more successful than Americans.

Our countrymen are the most discontented of mortals. They are always longing for "big strikes." If a "claim" is paying them a steady income, by which, if they pleased, they could lay up more in a month, than they could accumulate in a year at home, still, they are dissatisfied, and, in most cases, will wander off in search of better "diggings." There are hundreds now pursuing this foolish course, who, if they had stopped where they first "camped," would now have been rich men. Sometimes, a company of these wanderers will find itself upon a bar, where a few pieces of the precious metal lie scattered upon the surface of the ground; of course they immediately "prospect" it, which is accomplished, by "panning out" a few basinsful of the soil. If it "pays," they "claim" the spot, and build their shanties; the news spreads that wonderful "diggings" have been discovered at such a place,—the monte-dealers, those worse than fiends, rush vulture-like upon the scene and erect a round tent, where, in gambling, drinking, swearing and fighting, the *many* reproduce Pandemonium in more than its original horror, while a *few* honestly and industriously commence digging for gold, and lo! as if a fairy's wand had been waved above the bar, a full-grown mining town hath sprung into existence.

But first, let me explain to you the "claiming" system. As there are no State laws upon the subject, each mining community is permitted to make its own. Here, they have decided that no man may "claim" an area of more than forty feet square. This he "stakes off" and puts a notice upon it, to the effect that he "holds" it for mining purposes. If he does not choose to "work it" immediately, he is obliged to renew the notice every ten days; for without this precaution, any other person has a right to "jump it," that is, to take it from him. There are many ways of evading the above law. For instance, an individual can "hold" as many "claims" as he pleases, if he keeps a man at work in each, for this workman represents the original owner. I am told, however, that the laborer, himself, can "jump" the "claim" of the very man who employs him, if he pleases so to do. This is seldom, if ever, done; the person who is willing to be hired, generally prefers to receive the six dollars *per diem*, of which he is *sure* in any case, to running the risk of a "claim" not proving valuable. After all, the "holding of claims" by proxy is considered rather as a carrying out of the spirit of the law, than as an evasion of it. But there are many ways of *really* outwitting this rule, though I cannot stop now to relate them, which give rise to innumerable arbitrations, and nearly every Sunday, there is a "miners' meeting" connected with this subject.

Having got our gold mines discovered, and "claimed," I will try to give you a faint idea of how they "work" them. Here, in the mountains, the labor of excavation is extremely difficult, on account of the immense rocks which form a large portion of the soil. Of course, no man can "work out" a "claim" alone. For that reason, and also for the same that makes partnerships desirable, they congregate in companies of four or six, generally designating themselves by the name of the place from whence the majority of the members have emigrated; as for example, the "Illinois," "Bunker Hill," "Bay State," etc., companies. In many places the surface-soil, or in mining-phrase, the "top dirt," "pays" when worked in a "Long Tom." This machine, (I have never been able to discover the derivation of its name,) is a trough, generally about twenty feet in length, and eight inches in depth, formed of wood, with the exception of six feet at one end, called the "riddle,"

(query, why riddle?) which is made of sheet-iron, perfora-
ted with holes about the size of a large marble. Under-
neath this cullender-like portion of the "long-tom," is
placed another trough, about ten feet long, the sides six
inches perhaps in height, which divided through the middle by a slender slat, is called the "riffle-box." It takes
several persons to manage, properly, a "long-tom." Three
or four men station themselves with spades, at the head of
the machine, while at the foot of it, stands an individual
armed "wid de shovel and de hoe." The spadesmen throw
in large quantities of the precious dirt, which is washed
down to the "riddle" by a stream of water leading into the
"long-tom" through wooden gutters or "sluices." When
the soil reaches the "riddle," it is kept constantly in motion by the man with the hoe. Of course, by this means, all
the dirt and gold escapes through the perforations into the
"riffle-box" below, one compartment of which is placed
just beyond the "riddle." Most of the dirt washes over the
sides of the "riffle-box," but the gold being so astonishingly heavy remains safely at the bottom of it. When the
machine gets too full of stones to be worked easily, the
man whose business it is to attend to them throws them
out with his shovel, looking carefully among them as he
does so for any pieces of gold, which may have been too
large to pass through the holes of the "riddle." I am sorry
to say that he generally loses his labor. At night they "pan
out" the gold, which has been collected in the "riffle-
box" during the day. Many of the miners decline washing
the "top dirt" at all, but try to reach as quickly as possible
the "bed-rock," where are found the richest deposits of
gold. The river is supposed to have formerly flowed over
this "bed-rock," in the "crevices" of which, it left, as it
passed away, the largest portions of the so eagerly sought
for ore. The group of mountains amidst which we are liv-

ing is a spur of the Sierra Nevada; and the "bed-rock,"
(which in this vicinity is of slate) is said to run through the
entire range, lying, in distance varying from a few feet to
eighty or ninety, beneath the surface of the soil. On Indian Bar, the "bed-rock" falls in almost perpendicular
"benches," while at Rich Bar, the friction of the river has
formed it into large, deep basins, in which the gold, instead of being found, as you would naturally suppose, in
the bottom of it, lies for the most part, just below the rim.
A good-natured individual bored *me*, and tired *himself*, in
a hopeless attempt to make me comprehend that this was
only a necessary consequence of the under-current of the
water; but with my usual stupidity upon such matters, I
got but a vague idea from his scientific explanation, and
certainly shall not mystify *you*, with my confused notions
thereupon.

When a company wish to reach the bed rock as quickly
as possible, they "sink a shaft," (which is nothing more
nor less than digging a well,) until they "strike" it. They
then commence "drifting coyote holes" (as they call
them) in search of "crevices," which, as I told you before,
often pay immensely. These "coyote holes" sometimes
extend hundreds of feet into the side of the hill. Of course
they are obliged to use lights in working them. They generally proceed, until the air is so impure as to extinguish
the lights, when they return to the entrance of the excavation, and commence another, perhaps close to it. When
they think that a "coyote hole" has been faithfully
"worked," they "clean it up," which is done by scraping
the surface of the "bed rock" with a knife,—lest by chance
thay have overlooked a "crevice,"—and they are often
richly rewarded for this precaution.

Now I must tell you how those having "claims" on the
hills procure the water for washing them. The expense of

raising it in any way from the river, is too enormous to be thought of for a moment. In most cases it is brought from ravines in the mountains. A company, to which a friend of ours belongs, has dug a ditch about a foot in width and depth, and more than three miles in length, which is fed in this way. I wish that you could see this ditch. I never beheld a NATURAL streamlet more exquisitely beautiful. It undulates over the mossy roots, and the gray, old rocks, like a capricious snake, singing all the time a low song with the "liquidest murmur," and one might almost fancy it the airy and coquettish Undine herself. When it reaches the top of the hill, the sparkling thing is divided into five or six branches, each one of which supplies one, two, or three "long-toms." There is an extra one, called the "waste-ditch," leading to the river, into which the water is shut off at night and on Sundays. This "race" (another and peculiar name for it) has already cost the company more than five thousand dollars. They sell the water to others at the following rates: Those that have the first use of it pay ten per cent. upon all the gold that they take out. As the water runs off from their machine, (it now goes by the elegant name of "tailings,") it is taken by a company lower down; and as it is not worth so much as when it was clear, the latter pay but seven per cent. If any others wish the "tailings," now still less valuable than at first, they pay four per cent. on all the gold which they take out, be it much or little. The water companies are constantly in trouble, and the arbitrations on that subject are very frequent.

I think that I gave you a vague idea of "fluming" in a former letter; I will not, therefore, repeat it here, but will merely mention, that the numerous "fluming companies have already commenced their extensive operations upon the river.

As to the "rockers," so often mentioned in story and in song, I have not spoken of them since I commenced this letter. The truth is, that I have seldom seen them used, though hundreds are lying ownerless along the banks of the river. I suppose that other machines are better adapted to mining operations in the mountains.

Gold mining is Nature's great lottery scheme. A man may work in a claim for many months, and be poorer at the end of the time than when he commenced; or he may "take out" thousands in a few hours. It is a mere matter of chance. A friend of ours, a young Spanish surgeon from Guatemala, a person of intelligence and education, told us that, after "working a claim" for six months, he had taken out but six ounces.

It must be acknowledged, however, that if a person "work his claim" himself, is economical and industrious, keeps his health, and is satisfied with small gains, he is "bound" to make money. And yet, I cannot help remarking, that almost all with whom we are acquainted seem to have *lost*. Some have had their "claims" jumped; many holes which had been excavated, and prepared for working at a great expense, caved in during the heavy rains of the fall and winter. Often after a company has spent an immense deal of time and money in "sinking a shaft," the water from the springs, (the greatest obstacle which the miner has to contend with in this vicinity) rushes in so fast, that it is impossible to work in them, or to contrive any machinery to keep it out, and for that reason only, men have been compelled to abandon places where they were at the very time "taking out" hundreds of dollars a day. If a fortunate or an unfortunate (which shall I call him?) *does* happen to make a "big strike," he is almost sure to fall into the hands of the professed gamblers, who soon relieve him of all care of it. They have not troubled the Bar much during the winter, but as the spring opens, they flock in like ominous birds of prey. Last week one left here, after a stay of four days, with over a thousand dollars of the hard-earned gold of the miners. But enough of these best-beloved of Beelzebub, so infinitely worse than the robber or murderer;—for surely it would be kinder to take a man's life, than to poison him with the fatal passion for gambling.

Perhaps you would like to know what class of men is most numerous in the mines. As well as I can judge, there are upon this river as many foreigners as Americans. The former, with a few exceptions, are extremely ignorant and degraded; though we have the pleasure of being acquainted with three or four Spaniards of the highest education and accomplishments. Of the Americans, the majority are of the better class of mechanics. Next to these, in number, are the sailors and the farmers. There are a few merchants and steamboat-clerks, three or four physicians, and one lawyer. We have no ministers, though fourteen miles from here there is a "Rancho," kept by a man of distinguished appearance, an accomplished monte-dealer and horse-jockey, who is *said* to have been—in the States—a preacher of the Gospel. I know not if this be true; but at any rate, such things are not uncommon in California.

I have spun this letter out until my head aches dreadfully. How tiresome it is to write *sensible* (?) things! But I have one comfort,—though my epistle may not be interesting, you will not deny, dear M., that I have achieved my ambition of making it both commonplace and utilatory.

LETTER SIXTEENTH

RESIDENCE IN THE MINES

From our Log Cabin, Indian Bar,
May 1, 1852

YOU HAVE no idea, my good, little M., how reluctantly I
have seated myself to write to you. The truth is, that my
last tedious letter about mining and other tiresome things
has completely exhausted my scribbling powers, and from
that hour to this the epistolary spirit has never moved me
forward. Whether on that important occasion, my small
brain received a shock from which it will never recover, or
whether it is pure, physical laziness, which influenced me,
I know not; but this is certain, that no whipt school-boy
ever crept to his hated task more unwillingly, than I to my
writing desk on this beautiful morning. Perhaps my indis-
position to soil paper in your behalf is caused by the bewildering scent of that great, glorious bouquet of flowers,
which, gathered in the crisp mountain air, is throwing off
cloud after cloud ("each cloud *faint* with the fragrance it
bears,") of languid sweetness, filling the dark old room
with incense, and making of it a temple of beauty; like
those pure, angelic souls, which, irradiating a plain countenance, often render it more lovely than the chiseled
finish of the most perfect features.

O, Molly! how I wish that I could send you this jar of
flowers, containing, as it does, many which in New
England are rare exotics. Here, you will find in richest profusion the fine lady elegance of the syringa; there, glorious, white lilies, so pure and stately; the delicate yet robust beauty of the exquisite privet; irises of every hue and

size; and, prettiest of all, a sweet, snow-tinted flower, looking like immense clusters of seed pearl, which the Spaniards call *libla*. But the marvel of the group, is an orange-colored blossom, of a most rare and singular fragrance, growing somewhat in the style of the flox; this, with some branches of pink bloom of incomparable sweetness, is entirely new to me. Since I have commenced writing, one of the Doctor's patients has brought me a bunch of wild roses. O! how vividly at the sight of them started up before me those wooded valleys of the Connecticut, with their wondrous depths of foliage, which for a few weeks in midsummer, are perhaps unsurpassed in beauty by any in the world. I have arranged the dear *home* blossoms with a handful of flowers which were given to me this morning by an unknown Spaniard. They are shaped like an anemone, of the opaque whiteness of the magnolia, with a large spot of glittering blackness at the bottom of each petal. But enough of our mountain earth stars; it would take me all day to describe their "infinite variety."

Nothing of importance has happened since I last wrote, except that the Kanaka wife of a man living at the Junction has made him the happy father of a son and heir. They say that she is quite a pretty little woman, only fifteen years old, and walked all the way from Sacramento to this place.

A few evenings ago, a Spaniard was stabbed by an American. It seems that the presumptuous foreigner had the impertinence, to ask very humbly and meekly that most noble representative of the stars and stripes, if the latter would pay him a few dollars which he had owed him for some time. His high mightiness, the Yankee, was not going to put up with any such impertinence, and the poor Spaniard received, for answer, several inches of cold steel in his breast, which inflicted a very dangerous wound. Nothing was done, and very little was said about this atrocious affair.

At Rich Bar they have passed a set of resolutions for the guidance of the inhabitants during the summer; one of which is to the effect that no foreigner shall work in the mines on that Bar. This has caused nearly all the Spaniards to immigrate upon Indian Bar, and several new houses for the sale of liquor etc., are building by these people. It seems to me that the above law is selfish, cruel and narrow-minded in the extreme.

When I came here, the Humboldt was the only public house on the Bar. Now there are the "Oriental," "Golden Gate," "Don Juan," and four or five others, the names of which I do not know. On Sundays, the swearing, drinking, gambling and fighting, which are carried on in some of these houses, are truly horrible.

It is extremely healthy, here; with the exception of two or three men who were drowned when the river was so high, I have not heard of a death for months.

Nothing worth wasting ink upon has occurred for some time, except the capture of two grizzly bear cubs by the immortal "Yank." He shot the mother, but she fell over the side of a steep hill, and he lost her. "Yank" intends to tame one of the cubs; the other he sold, I believe, for fifty dollars. They are certainly the funniest looking things that I ever saw, and the oddest possible pets.

By the way, we receive an echo from the outer world once a month, and the expressman never fails to bring three letters from my dear M. wherewith to gladden the heart of her sister, "Dame Shirley."

May 25

THE VERY day after I last wrote you, dear M., a troop of mules came on to the Bar, bringing us almost forgotten luxuries, in the form of potatoes, onions and butter. A band of these animals is always a pretty sight, and you can imagine that the solemn fact of our having been destitute of the abovementioned edibles since the middle of February, did not detract from the pleasure with which we saw them winding cautiously down the hill, stepping daintily here and there with those absurd little feet of theirs, and appearing so extremely anxious for the safe conveyance of their loads. They belonged to a Spanish packer; were in excellent condition, sleek and fat as so many kittens, and of every possible color,—black, white, grey, sorrel, cream, brown, etc. Almost all of them had some bit of red, or blue, or yellow, about their trappings, which added not a little to the brilliancy of their appearance; while the gay tinkle of the leader's bell, mingling with those shrill and peculiar exclamations, with which Spanish muleteers are in the habit of urging on their animals, made a not un-pleasing medley of sounds. But the creamiest part of the whole affair was—I must confess it, unromantic as it may seem—when the twenty-five or thirty pretty creatures were collected into the small space between our cabin and the Humboldt; such a gathering together of ham and mackerel-fed bipeds—such a lavish display of gold dust—such troops of happy looking men, bending beneath the delicious weight of butter and potatoes—and above all, *such* a smell of fried onions, as instantaneously rose upon the fragrant California air, and ascended gratefully into the blue California Heaven, was, I think, never experienced before.

On the first of May a train had arrived at Rich Bar; and on the morning of the day which I have been describing to you, one of our friends arose some three hours earlier than usual, went over to the aforesaid Bar, bought twenty-five pounds of potatoes at forty cents a pound, and packed them home on his back. In less than two days afterwards, half a dozen cargoes had arrived, and the same vegetable was selling at a shilling a pound. The trains had been on the road several weeks, but the heavy showers, which had continued almost daily through the month of April, had retarded their arrival.

Last week I rode on horseback to a beautiful Bar called the Junction, so named from the fact that at that point the East Branch of the North Fork of the Feather River unites itself with the main North Fork. The mule trail, which lies along the verge of a dreadful precipice, is three or four miles long, while the foot-path leading by the river is not more than two miles in length. The latter is impassable, on account of the log bridges having been swept away by the recent freshets. The other day two oxen lost their footing, and fell over the precipice; and it is the general opinion that they were killed long before they reached the golden palace of the Plumerian Thetis. I was a little alarmed at first, for fear my horse would stumble, in which case I should have shared the fate of the unhappy beeves, but soon forgot all fear in the enchanting display of flowers which each opening in the shrubs displayed to me. "Earth's firmament" was starred with daphnes, irises and violets of every hue and size; pale wood anemones,

with but one faint sigh of fragrance as they expired, died
by hundreds beneath my horse's tread; and spotted tiger-
lilies, with their stately heads all bedizened in orange and
black, marshaled along the path like an army of gaily-clad
warriors. But the flowers are not all of an Oriental character. Do you remember, Molly, dear, how you and I once
quarreled when we were—oh! such mites of children—
about a sprig of syringa? The dear mother was obliged to
interfere, and to make all right, she gave you a small
brown bud of most penetrating fragrance, which she told
you was much more valuable than the contested flower. I
remember perfectly that she failed entirely in convincing
me that the dark, somber flower was half as beautiful as
my pretty, cream-tinted blossom; and, if I mistake not,
you were but poutingly satisfied with the substitute.
Here, even if we retained, which I do not, our childish fas-
cination for syringas, we should not need to quarrel about
them, for they are as common as dandelions in a New
England meadow, and dispense their peculiar perfume—
which, by the way, always reminds me of Lubin's choicest
scents—in almost sickening profusion. Besides the abovementioned flowers, we saw wild roses, and buttercups,
and flox, and privet, and whole acres of the "Wandlike
lily." I have often heard it said, though I cannot vouch for
the truth of the assertion, that it is only during the month
of January that you cannot gather a bouquet in the mountains.

Just before one reaches the Junction, there is a beautiful grove of oaks, through which there leaps a gay little
rivulet, celebrated for the grateful coolness of its waters.
Of course, one is expected to propitiate this pretty Undine by drinking a draught of her glittering waters from a
dirty tin cup, which some benevolent cold-water man has
suspended from a tree near the spring. The bank leading

down into the stream is so steep that people generally dismount and lead their animals across it. But F. declared that I was so light that the horse could easily carry me, and insisted upon my keeping the saddle. Of course, like a dutiful wife, I had nothing to do but to obey. So I grasped firmly the reins, shut my eyes, and committed myself to the Fates that take care of thistle seeds, and lo! the next moment I found myself safely on the other side of the brook; my pretty steed—six weeks ago he was an Indian pony running wild in the prairie—curveting about and arching his elegant neck, evidently immensely proud of the grace and ease with which he had conveyed his burden across the brook. In a few moments we alighted at the store, which is owned by some friends of F., whom we found looking like so many great daisies, in their new shirts of pink calico, which had been donned in honor of our expected arrival.

The Junction is the most beautiful of all the Bars. From the store, one can walk nearly a mile down the river quite easily. The path is bordered by a row of mingled oaks and firs—the former garlanded with mistletoe, and the latter embroidered with that exquisitely beautiful moss which I tried to describe in one of my first letters.

The little Kanaka woman lives here. I went to see her. She is quite pretty—with large, lustrous eyes, and two great braids of hair, which made me think of black satin cables, they were so heavy and massive. She has good teeth, a sweet smile, and a skin not much darker than that of a French brunette. I never saw any creature so proud as she, almost a child herself, was of her baby. In jest, I asked her to give it to me, and really was almost alarmed at the vehement burst of tears with which she responded to my request. Her husband explained the cause of her distress. It is a superstition among her people that he who refuses

to give another anything, no matter what—there are no exceptions which that other may ask for—will be over-
whelmed with the most dreadful misfortunes. Her own
parents had parted with her for the same reason. Her
pretty, girlish face soon resumed its smiles when I told her
that I was in jest, and, to console me for the disappoint-
ment which she thought I must feel at not obtaining her
little brown treasure, she promised to give me the *next*
one! It is a Kanaka custom to make a present to the person
calling upon them for the first time; in accordance with
which habit, I received a pair of dove-colored boots three
sizes too large for me.

I should like to have visited the Indian encampment,
which lies a few miles from the Junction, but was too
much fatigued to attempt it. The Indians often visit us,
and as they seldom wear anything but a *very* tight and
very short shirt, they have an appearance of being, as
Charles Dickens would say, all legs. They usually sport
some kind of a head-dress, if it is nothing more than a
leather string, which they bind across their dusky brows in
the style of the wreaths in Norma, or the gay ribbons gar-
landing the hair of the Roman youth in the play of Brutus.
A friend of ours, who has visited their camp several times,
has just given me a description of their mode of life. Their
huts, ten or twelve in number, are formed of the bark of
the pine—conically shaped, plastered with mud, and with
a hole in the top, whence emerges the smoke, which rises
from a fire built in the center of the apartment. These
places are so low that it is quite impossible to stand upright in them, and are entered from a small hole in one
side, on all fours. A large stone, sunk to its surface in the
ground, which contains three or four pan-like hollows for
the purpose of grinding acorns and nuts, is the only furniture which these huts contain. The women, with another

stone, about a foot and a half in length, and a little larger than a man's wrist, pulverize the acorns to the finest possible powder, which they prepare for the table (?) in the following manner, viz:—Their cooking utensils consist of a kind of basket, woven of some particular species of reed, I should fancy, from the descriptions which I have had of them, and are so plaited as to be impervious to fluids. These they fill half full of water, which is made to boil by placing in it hot stones. The latter they drag from the fire with two sticks. When the water boils, they stir into it, until it is about as thick as hasty-pudding, the powdered acorns, delicately flavored with dried grasshoppers, and lo! dinner is ready. Would you like to know how they eat? They place the thumb and little finger together across the palm of the hand, and make of the other three fingers a spoon, with which they shovel into their capacious mouths this delicious compound.

There are about eighty Indians in all at this encampment, a very small portion of which number are women. A hostile tribe in the valley made a Sabine-like invasion upon the settlement, a few months since, and stole away all the young and fair *muchachas*, leaving them but a few old squaws. These poor, withered creatures, who are seldom seen far from the encampment, do all the drudgery. Their entire wardrobe consists of a fringe about two feet in length, which is formed of the branch or root—I cannot ascertain exactly which—of a peculiar species of shrub shredded into threads. This scanty costume they festoon several times about the person, fastening it just above the hips, and they generally appear in a startlingly unsophisticated state of almost entire nudity. They are very filthy in their habits; and my informant said that if one of them should venture out into the rain, grass would grow on her neck and arms. The men, unhappy martyrs! are compelled to be a little more cleanly, from their custom of hunting and fishing, for the wind *will* blow off *some* of the dirt, and the water washes off more.

Their infants are fastened to a framework of light wood in the same manner as those of the North American Indians. When a squaw has anything to do, she very composedly sets this frame up against the side of the house, as a civilized housewife would an umbrella or broom.

Some of their modes of fishing are very curious. One is as follows: These primitive anglers will seek a quiet, deep spot in the river, where they know fish "most do congregate," and throw therein a large quantity of stones. This, of course, frightens the fish, which dive to the bottom of the stream, and Mr. Indian, plunging headforemost into the water, beneath which he sometimes remains several minutes, will presently reappear, holding triumphantly in each hand one of the finny tribe, which he kills by giving it a single bite in the head or neck with his sharp, knife-like teeth.

Hardly a day passes during which there are not three or four of them on this Bar. They often come into the cabin, and I never order them away, as most others do, for their childish curiosity amuses me, and as yet they have not been troublesome. There is one beautiful little boy about eight years old, who generally accompanies them. We call him Wild Bird, for he is as shy as a partridge, and we have never yet been able to coax him into the cabin. He always wears a large, red shirt, which, trailing to his little bronzed feet, and the sleeves every other minute dropping down over his dusky models of hands, gives him a very odd appearance. One day Mrs. B., whom I was visiting at the time, coaxed Wild Bird into the house to see Charley, the hero of the champagne-basket cradle. The little fellow gazed at us with his large, startled eyes, without showing the least shadow of fear in his countenance; but his heart beat so violently that we could actually see the rise and fall of the old red shirt which covered its tremblings. Mrs. B. made our copper-colored cupidon a pretty suit of crimson calico. His protectors, half a dozen grim old Indians, (it was impossible to tell which was his father, they all made such a petted darling of him,) were compelled to array him in his new suit by main strength, he screaming dreadfully all the time. Indeed, so exhausted was he by his shrieks, that by the time he was fairly buttoned up in his crimson trappings, he sank on the ground in a deep sleep. The next day the barbarous little villain appeared trailing, as usual, his pet shirt after him at every step, while the dandy jacket and the trim baby trowsers had vanished we never knew whither.

The other morning an Indian appeared on the Bar robed from neck to heels in a large, white sheet, and you have no idea of the classic grace with which he had arranged the folds about his fine person. We at first thought him a woman, and he himself was in an ecstasy of glee at our mistake.

It is impossible to conceive of anything more light and airy than the step of these people. I shall never forget with what enchanted eyes I gazed upon one of them gliding along the side of the hill opposite Missouri Bar. One would fancy that nothing but a fly or a spirit could keep its footing on the rocks along which he stepped so stately, for they looked as perpendicular as a wall. My friend observed that no white man could have done it. This wild creature seemed to move as a cloud moves on a quiet day in summer, and as still and silently. It really made me solemn to gaze upon him, and the sight almost impressed me as something superhuman.

Viewed in the most favorable manner, these poor creatures are miserably brutish and degraded having very little in common with the lofty and eloquent aborigines of the United States. It is said that their entire language contains but about twenty words. Like all Indians, they are passionately fond of gambling, and will exhibit as much anxiety at the losing or winning of a handful of beans as do their paler brothers when thousands are at stake. Methinks, from what I have seen of that most hateful vice, the *amount* lost or won has very little to do with the matter. But let me not speak of this most detestable of crimes. I have known such frightful consequences to ensue from its indulgence, that I dare not speak of it, lest I use language, as perhaps I have already done, unbecoming a woman's lips.

Hundreds of people have arrived upon our Bar within the last few days; drinking saloons are springing up in every direction; the fluming operations are rapidly progressing, and all looks favorably for a busy and prosperous summer to our industrious miners.

RESIDENCE IN THE MINES

From our Log Cabin, Indian Bar,
July 5, 1852

DEAR M:—Our Fourth of July celebration, which came off at Rich Bar, was quite a respectable affair. I had the honor of making a flag for the occasion. The stripes were formed of cotton cloth and red calico, of which last gorgeous material, no possible place in California is ever destitute. A piece of drilling, taken from the roof of the Humboldt, which the rain and the sun had faded from its original, somber hue, to just that particular shade of blue, which you and I admire so much—served for a Union. A large star in the center, covered with gold leaf, represented California. Humble as were the materials of which it was composed, this banner made quite a gay appearance, floating from the top of a lofty pine, in front of the Empire, to which it was suspended.

I went over to Rich Bar at six in the morning, not wishing to take so fatiguing a walk in the heat of the day. After breakfast, I assisted Mrs. B. and one of the gentlemen, in decorating the dining-room; the walls of which, we completely covered with grape-vines, relieved here and there, with bunches of elder-blow. We made several handsome bouquets, and arranged one of syringas, white lilies and the feathery green of the cedar, to be presented, in the name of the ladies, to the Orator of the Day. You can imagine my disgust, when the ceremony was performed, to observe that some officious Goth, had marred the perfect keeping of the gift, by thrusting into the vase, several ugly, purple blossoms.

The exercises were appointed to commence at ten o'clock, but they were deferred for half an hour, in expectation of the arrival of two ladies, who had taken up their abode in the place within the last six weeks, and were living on Indian Bar Hill. As they did not come, however, it was thought necessary to proceed without them; so Mrs. B. and myself, were obliged to sit upon the piazza of the Empire, comprising in our two persons, the entire female audience.

The scene was indeed striking. The green, garlanded hills girdling Rich Bar, looked wonderfully beautiful, rising with their grand, abrupt outlines into the radiant summer sky. A platform reared in front of the Empire, beneath the banner-tasseled pine, and arched with fragrant fir-boughs, made the prettiest possible rustic rostrum. The audience, grouped beneath the awnings of the different shops, dressed in their colored shirts,—though here and there, one might observe a dandy miner, who had relieved the usual vestment, by placing beneath it one of calico or white muslin—added much to the picturesqueness of the scene. Unfortunately, the Committee of Arrangements had not been able to procure a copy of the Declaration of Independence. Its place was supplied by an apologetic speech from a Mr. J., who will, without doubt, be the Democratic candidate for State Representative at the coming election. This gentleman finished his performance, by introducing Mr. B., the Orator of the Day, who is the Whig nominee for the abovementioned office. Be-

fore pronouncing his Address, Mr. B. read some verses,
which he said had been handed to him anonymously, the
evening before. I have copied them for your amusement.
They are as follows, and are entitled—

A FOURTH OF JULY WELCOME TO THE MINERS

Ye are welcome, merry miners! in your blue and red
  shirts, all!
Ye are welcome, 'mid these golden hills, to your Nation's
  Festival;
Though ye've not shaved your savage lips, nor cut your
  barbarous hair—
Ye are welcome, merry miners! all bearded as ye are.

What, though your brows are blushing, at the kisses of the
  sun,
And your once white and well-kept hands, are stained a
  sober dun;
What though your backs are bent with toil, and ye have
  lost the air,
With which ye bowed your stately heads, amid the young
  and fair,

I fain would in my slender palm your horny fingers clasp,
For I love the hand of honest toil, its firm and heartfelt
  grasp;
And I know, Oh miners, brave and true! that not alone for
  self,
Have ye heaped through many wearying months, your
  glittering pile of pelf.

Ye, of the dark and thoughtful eyes beneath the bronzed
  brow;

Ye, on whose smooth and rounded cheeks, still gleams
          youth's purple glow;
Ye of the reckless, daring life—ye, of the timid glance;
Ho! young and old; Ho! grave and gay, to our Nation's
          fete advance.

Ho! sun-kissed brother from the South, where radiant
          skies are glowing;
Ho! toiler from the stormy North, where snowy winds are
          blowing;
Ho! Buckeye, Hoosier, from the West, sons of the river
          great—
Come shout Columbia's birthday song, in the new Golden
          State.

Ho! children of imperial France; Ho! Erin's brave and
          true;
Ho! England's golden bearded race—we fain would wel-
          come you;
And dark-eye'd friends from those glad climes, where
          Spain's proud blood is seen—
To join in Freedom's holy psalm, ye'll not refuse, I ween.

For now the banner of the free is in *very deed* our own,
And 'mid the brotherhood of States, not ours, the feeblest
          one.
Then proudly shout, ye bushy men, with throats all
          brown and bare,
For lo! from 'midst our flag's brave blue, leaps out a
          golden star.

After reading the above lines, Mr. B. pronounced beautifully a very splendid Oration. Unlike such efforts in general, it was exceedingly fresh and new; so that instead of
its being that infliction that Fourth of July Orations com-

monly are, it was a high pleasure to listen to him. Perhaps,
where Nature herself is so original, it is impossible for even
thought to be hackneyed. It is too long for a letter, but as
the miners have requested a copy for publication, I will
send it to you in print.

About half an hour after the close of the Oration, the
ladies from the hill arrived. They made a pretty picture
descending the steep, the one with her wealth of floating
curls turbaned in a snowy nubie, and her white dress set
off by a crimson scarf; the other, with a little Pamella hat,
placed coquettishly upon her brown, braided tresses, and
a magnificent Chinese shawl enveloping her slender figure.
So lately arrived from the States, with everything fresh
and new, they quite extinguished poor Mrs. B. and myself,
trying our best to look fashionable in our antique mode of
four years ago.

The dinner was excellent. We had a real, live Captain, a
very gentlemanly person, who had actually been in action
during the Mexican War, for president. Many of the toasts
were quite spicy and original; one of the new ladies sang
three or four beautiful songs, and everything passed off at
Rich Bar quite respectably. To be sure, there was a small
fight in the bar-room—which is situated just below the
dining-room—during which much speech and a little
blood were spouted; whether the latter catastrophe was
caused by a blow received, or the large talking of the victim, is not known. Two peacefully inclined citizens who,
at the first battle-shout, had rushed manfully to the rescue, returned at the subsiding of hostilities with blood-
bespattered shirt-bosoms; at which fearful sight, the
pretty wearer of the Pamella hat—one of the delinquents
being her husband—chose to go faint, and would not
finish her dinner, which, as we saw that her distress was
real, somewhat marred our enjoyment.

On our way home, half a dozen gentlemen, who pre-

ceded us, stepped in front of a cabin, full of "Infant Phenomena," and gave nine cheers for "the mother and her
children;" which will show what a rarity those embodi-
ments of noise and disquiet are in the mountains. This
group of pretty darlings consists of three sweet little girls,
slender, straight, and white as ivory wands, moving with
an incessant and *staccato* (do you remember our old
music lessons?) activity, which always makes me think of
my humming birds.

About five o'clock, we arrived at home, just in time to
hear some noisy shouts of "Down with the Spaniards;"
"The great American People forever," and other similar
cries, evident signs of quite a spirited fight between the
two parties, which was, in reality, taking place at the moment. Seven or eight of the *elite* of Rich Bar, drunk with
whisky and patriotism, were the principal actors in this
unhappy affair, which resulted in serious injury to two or
three Spaniards. For some time past, there has been a
gradually increasing state of bad feeling exhibited by our
countrymen (increased, we fancy, by the ill-treatment
which our Consul received the other day at Acapulco,) towards foreigners. In this affair, our own countrymen were
principally to blame, or, rather I should say, Sir Barley
Corn was to blame, for many of the ringleaders are fine
young men, who, when sober, are decidedly friendly to
the Spaniards. It is feared that this will not be the end of
the fracas, though the more intelligent foreigners, as well
as the judicious Americans, are making every effort to
promote kindly feeling between the two nations. This will
be very difficult, on account of the ignorant prejudices of
the low-bred, which class are a large proportion of both
parties.

It is very common to hear vulgar Yankees say of the
Spaniards, "Oh, they are half-civilized black men!" These

unjust expressions naturally irritate the latter, many of
whom are highly educated gentlemen of the most refined
and cultivated manners. We labor under great disadvan-
tages, in the judgment of foreigners. Our peculiar, politi-
cal institutions, and the prevalence of common schools,
give to *all* our people an arrogant assurance, which is mistaken for the American *beau ideal* of a gentleman.

They are unable to distinguish those nice *shades* of
manner, which as effectually separate the gentleman from
the clown with *us*, as do these broader lines, which mark
these two classes among all other nations. They think that
it is the grand characteristic of Columbia's children, to be
prejudiced, opinionated, selfish, avaricious and unjust. It
is vain to tell them, that such are not specimens of American gentlemen. They will answer, "They call themselves
gentlemen, and you receive them in your houses as such."
It is utterly impossible for foreigners to thoroughly comprehend and make due allowance for that want of delicacy, and that vulgar "I'm as good as you are," spirit,
which is, it must be confessed, peculiar to the lower
classes of our people, and which would lead the majority
of them to—

> "Enter a palace with their old felt hat on—
> To address the King with the title of Mister,
> And ask him the price of the throne he sat on."

The class of men who rule society (?) in the mines, are the
gamblers, who, for the most part, are reckless, bad men,
although no doubt there are many among them, whose
only vice is that fatal love of play. The rest of the people
are afraid of these daring, unprincipled persons, and when
they commit the most glaring injustice against the Spaniards, it is generally passed unnoticed.

We have had innumerable drunken fights during the summer, with the usual amount of broken heads, collar bones, stabs, etc. Indeed, the sabbaths are almost always enlivened by some such merry event. Were it not for these affairs, I might sometimes forget that the sweet day of rest was shining down upon us.

Last week, the dead body of a Frenchman was found in the river, near Missouri Bar. On examination of the body, it was the general opinion that he had been murdered. Suspicion has, as yet, fallen upon no person.

LETTER NINETEENTH

RESIDENCE IN THE MINES

From our Log Cabin, Indian Bar,
August 4, 1852

WE HAVE lived through so much excitement for the last three weeks, dear M., that I almost shrink from relating the gloomy events which have marked their flight. But if I leave out the darker shades of our mountain life, the picture will be very incomplete. In the short space of twenty-four days, we have had murders, fearful accidents, bloody deaths, a mob, whippings, a hanging, an attempt at suicide, and a fatal duel. But to begin at the beginning, as according to rule one ought to do.

I think that even among these beautiful hills, I never saw a more perfect "bridal of the earth and sky," than that of Sunday the eleventh of July. On that morning, I went with a party of friends to the head of the "Ditch," a walk of about three miles in length. I do not believe that Nature herself ever made anything so lovely, as this artificial brooklet. It glides like a living thing, through the very heart of the forest; sometimes creeping softly on, as though with muffled feet, through a wilderness of aquatic plants; sometimes dancing gaily over a white pebbled bottom; now making a "sunshine in a shady place," across the mossy roots of the majestic old trees—and anon leaping with a grand anthem, adown the great, solemn rocks, which lie along its beautiful pathway. A sunny opening at the head of the ditch, is a garden of perfumed shrubbery and many-tinted flowers—all garlanded with the prettiest vines imaginable, and peopled with an infinite variety of magnificent butterflies. These last were of every possible color—pink, blue and yellow, shining black splashed with orange, purple fleshed with gold, white, and even green. We returned about three in the evening, loaded with fragrant bundles, which arranged in jars, tumblers, pitcher, bottles and pails, (we are not particular as to the quality of our vases in the mountains, and love our flowers as well in their humble chalices as if their beautiful heads lay against a background of marble or porcelain,) made the dark old cabin, "a bower of beauty for us."

Shortly after our arrival, a perfectly deafening volley of shouts and yells elicited from my companion the careless remark, "that the customary Sabbath-day's fight was apparently more serious than usual." Almost as he spoke, there succeeded a death-like silence, broken in a minute after by a deep groan, at the corner of the cabin, followed by the words, "Why Tom, poor fellow, are you really wounded?" Before we could reach the door, it was burst violently open, by a person who inquired hurriedly for the Doctor—who, luckily, happened at that very moment to be approaching. The man who called him, then gave us the following excited account of what had happened. He said that in a *mele* between the Americans and the foreigners, D o mingo—a tall, majestic-looking Spaniard, a perfect type of the novelistic bandit of Old Spain—had stabbed Tom Somers, a young Irishman, but a naturalized citizen of the United States—and that at the very moment, said Domingo, with a *Mejicana* hanging upon his arm, and brandishing threateningly the long, bloody knife with which he had inflicted the wound upon his victim, was parading up and down the street unmolested. It seems that when Tom Somers fell, the Americans, being unarmed, were seized with a sudden panic and fled. There was a rumor, (unfounded, as it afterwards proved) to the effect, that the Spaniards had on this day conspired to kill all the Americans on the river. In a few moments, however, the latter rallied and made a rush at the murderer, who immediately plunged into the river and swam across to Missouri Bar; eight or ten shots were fired at him while in the water, not one of which hit him. He ran like an antelope across the flat, swam thence to Smith's Bar, and escaped by the road leading out of the mountains, from the Junction. Several men went in pursuit of him, but he was not taken, and without doubt, is now safe in Mexico.

In the meanwhile, the consternation was terrific. The Spaniards, who, with the exception of six or eight, knew no more of the affair than I did, thought that the Americans had arisen against them; and our own countrymen equally ignorant, fancied the same of the foreigners. About twenty of the latter, who were either sleeping or reading in their cabins at the time of the *emeute*, aroused by the cry of "Down with the Spaniards!" barricaded themselves in a drinking-saloon, determined to defend themselves as long as possible, against the massacre, which was fully expected would follow this appalling shout. In the bake-shop, which stands next door to our cabin, young Tom Somers lay straightened for the grave, (he lived but fifteen minutes after he was wounded,) while over his dead body a Spanish woman, was weeping and moaning in the most piteous and heart-rending manner. The Rich Barians, who had heard a most exaggerated account of the rising of the Spaniards against the Americans, armed with rifles, pistols, clubs, dirks, etc., were rushing down the hill by hundreds. Each one added fuel to his rage, by crowding into the little bakery, to gaze upon the blood-bathed bosom of the victim, yet warm with the life, which but an hour before it had so triumphantly worn. Then arose the most fearful shouts of "Down with the

Spaniards!" "Drive every foreigner off the river!" "Don't
let one of the murderous devils remain." "Oh, if you have
a drop of American blood in your veins, it must cry out
for vengeance upon the cowardly assassins of poor Tom."
All this, mingled with the most horrible oaths and execra-
tions yelled up, as if in mockery, into that smiling heaven,
which in its fair Sabbath calm, bent unmoved over the hell
which was raging below.

After a time, the more sensible and sober part of the
community succeeding in quieting, in a partial degree, the
enraged and excited multitude. During the whole affair I
had remained perfectly calm, in truth, much more so than
I am now, when recalling it. The entire catastrophe had
been so unexpected, and so sudden in its consummation,
that I fancy I was stupefied into the most exemplary good
behavior. F. and several of his friends, taking advantage of
the lull in the storm, came into the cabin and entreated me
to join the two women who were living on the hill. At this
time, it seemed to be the general opinion, that there
would be a serious fight, and they said I might be
wounded accidentally, if I remained on the Bar. As I had
no fear of anything of the kind, I plead hard to be allowed
to stop, but when told that my presence would increase
the anxiety of our friends, of course, like a dutiful wife, I
went on to the hill.

We three women, left entirely alone, seated ourselves
upon a log, overlooking the strange scene below. The Bar,
was a sea of heads, bristling with guns, rifles and clubs. We
could see nothing, but fancied from the apparent quiet of
the crowd, that the miners were taking measures to inves-
tigate the sad event of the day. All at once, we were startled by the firing of a gun, and the next moment, the
crowd dispersing, we saw a man led into the log cabin,
while another was carried, apparently lifeless, into a Span-

ish drinking-saloon, from one end of which, were burst off instantly several boards, evidently to give air to the wounded person. Of course, we were utterly unable to imagine what had happened; and to all our perplexity and anxiety, one of the ladies insisted upon believing that it was her own husband who had been shot, and as she is a very nervous woman, you can fancy our distress. It was in vain to tell her—which we did over and over again—that that worthy individual wore a *blue* shirt, and the wounded person a *red* one; she doggedly insisted that her dear M. had been shot, and having informed us confidentially and rather inconsistently that "she should never see him again, never, never," plumped herself down upon the log in an attitude of calm and ladylike despair, which would have been infinitely amusing, had not the occasion been so truly a fearful one. Luckily for our nerves, a benevolent individual, taking pity upon our loneliness, came and told us what had happened.

It seems that an Englishman, the owner of a house of the vilest description, a person, who is said to have been the primary cause of all the troubles of the day, attempted to force his way through the line of armed men which had been formed at each side of the street. The guard very properly refused to let him pass. In his drunken fury, he tried to wrest a gun from one of them, which being accidentally discharged in the struggle, inflicted a severe wound upon a Mr. Oxley, and shattered in the most dreadful manner the thigh of Señor Pizarro, a man of high birth and breeding, a *porteño* of Buenos Ayres. This frightful accident recalled the people to their senses, and they began to act a little less like madmen, than they had previously done. They elected a Vigilance Committee, and authorized persons to go to the Junction and arrest the suspected Spaniards.

The first act of the Committee was to try a *Mejicana*, who had been foremost in the fray. She has always worn male attire, and on this occasion, armed with a pair of pistols, she fought like a very fury. Luckily, inexperienced in the use of fire-arms, she wounded no one. She was sentenced to leave the Bar by day-light, a perfectly just decision, for there is no doubt that she is a regular little demon. Some went so far as to say, she ought to be hung, for she was the *indirect* cause of the fight. You see always, it is the old, cowardly excuse of Adam in Paradise: "The *woman* tempted me, and I did eat." As if the poor, frail head, once so pure and beautiful, had not sin enough of its own, dragging it forever downward, without being made to answer for the wrong-doing of a whole community of men.

The next day, the Committee tried five or six Spaniards, who were proven to have been the ringleaders in the Sabbath-day riot. Two of them were sentenced to be whipped, the remainder to leave the Bar that evening; the property of all to be confiscated to the use of the wounded persons. Oh Mary! imagine my anguish when I heard the first blow fall upon those wretched men. I had never thought that I should be compelled to hear such fearful sounds, and, although I immediately buried my head in a shawl, nothing can efface from memory the disgust and horror of that moment. I had heard of such things, but heretofore had not realized, that in the nineteenth century, men could be beaten like dogs, much less that other men, not only could sentence such barbarism, but could actually stand by and see their own manhood degraded in such disgraceful manner. One of these unhappy persons was a very gentlemanly young Spaniard, who implored for death in the most moving terms. He appealed to his judges in the most eloquent manner—as gentlemen, as men of honor; representing to them that to

be deprived of life, was nothing in comparison with the
never-to-be-effaced stain of the vilest convict's punishment—to which they had sentenced him. Finding all his
entreaties disregarded, he swore a most solemn oath, that
he would murder every American that he should chance
to meet alone, and as he is a man of the most dauntless
courage, and rendered desperate by a burning sense of disgrace, which will cease only with his life, he will doubtless
keep his word.

Although in my very humble opinion and in that of
others more competent to judge of such matters than
myself, these sentences were unnecessarily severe, yet so
great was the rage and excitement of the crowd, that the
Vigilance Committee could do no less. The mass of the
mob demanded fiercely the death of the prisoners, and it
was evident that many of the Committee took side with
the people. I shall never forget how horror-struck I was
(bombastic as it *now* sounds) at hearing no less a personage than the Whig candidate for representative say, "that
the condemned had better fly for their lives, for the Aven-
ger of Blood was on their tracks!" I am happy to say, that
said very worthy, but sanguinary individual, "The Aven-
ger of Blood!" represented in this case by some half dozen
gambling rowdies, either changed his mind or lost scent of
his prey; for the intended victims slept about two miles up
the hill, quite peacefully until morning.

The following facts, elicited upon the trial, throw light
upon this unhappy affair: Seven miners from Old Spain,
enraged at the cruel treatment which their countrymen
had received on the "Fourth," and at the illiberal cry of
"Down with the Spaniard," had united for the purpose of
taking revenge on seven Americans whom they believed to
be the originators of their insults. All well armed, they
came from the Junction, where they were residing at the

time, intending to challenge each one his man, and in fair fight, compel their insolent aggressors to answer for the arrogance which they had exhibited more than once towards the Spanish race. Their first move on arriving at Indian Bar was to go and dine at the Humboldt, where they drank a most enormous quantity of champagne and claret. Afterwards, they proceeded to the house of the Englishman, whose brutal carelessness caused the accident which wounded Pizarro and Oxley, when one of them commenced a playful conversation with one of his countrywomen. This enraged the Englishman, who instantly struck the Spaniard a violent blow, and ejected him from the shanty. Thereupon ensued a spirited fight, which, through the exertion of a gentleman from Chili, a favorite with both nations, ended without bloodshed. This person knew nothing of the intended duel, or he might have prevented, by his wise counsels, what followed. Not suspecting for a moment anything of the kind, he went to Rich Bar. Soon after he left, Tom Somers, who is said always to have been a dangerous person when in liquor, without any apparent provocation, struck Domingo, (one of the original seven) a violent blow, which nearly felled him to the earth. The latter, a man of "dark antecedents" and the most reckless character, mad with wine, rage and revenge, without an instant's pause, drew his knife and inflicted a fatal wound upon his insulter. Thereupon followed the chapter of accidents which I have related.

On Tuesday following the fatal Sabbath, a man brought the news of the murder of a Mr. Bacon, a person well known on the river, who kept a ranch about twelve miles from Rich Bar. He was killed for his money, by his servant, a negro, who not three months ago was our own cook. He was the last one anybody would have suspected capable of such an act.

A party of men, appointed by the Vigilance Committee, left the Bar immediately in search of him. The miserable wretch was apprehended in Sacramento and part of
the gold found upon his person. On the following Sunday
he was brought in chains to Rich Bar. After a trial by the
miners, he was sentenced to be hung at four o'clock in the
evening. All efforts to make him confess proved futile. He
said, very truly, that whether innocent or guilty, they
would hang him; and so he "died and made no sign," with
a calm indifference, as the novelists say, "worthy of a
better cause." The dreadful crime and death of "Josh,"
who having been an excellent cook, and very neat and re-
spectful, was a favorite servant with us, added to the un-
happiness which you can easily imagine that I was suffering under all these horrors.

On Saturday evening about eight o'clock, as we sat
quietly conversing with the two ladies from the hill—who,
by the way, we found very agreeable additions to our society, hitherto composed entirely of gentlemen—we were
startled by the loud shouting, and rushing close by the
door of the cabin, which stood open, of three or four hundred men. Of course, we feminines, with nerves somewhat
shattered from the events of the past week, were greatly
alarmed.

We were soon informed that Henry Cook, *vice* "Josh"
had, in a fit of delirium tremens, cut his throat from ear to
ear. The poor wretch was alone when he committed the
desperate deed, and in his madness, throwing the bloody
razor upon the ground, he ran part of the way up the hill.
Here he was found almost senseless, and brought back to
the Humboldt, where he was very nearly the cause of
hanging poor "Paganini Ned"—who returned a few weeks
since from the valley,—for his first act on recovering himself, was to accuse that culinary individual of having attempted to murder him. The mob were for hanging our

poor "Vattel" without judge or jury, and it was only through the most strenuous exertions of his friends, that the life of this illustrious person was saved. Poor Ned! it was forty-eight hours before his cork-screws returned to their original graceful curl; he threatens to leave us to our barbarism and no longer to waste his culinary talents upon an ungrateful and inappreciative people. He has sworn "war to the knife" against Henry, who was formerly his most intimate friend, as nothing can persuade him that the accusation did not proceed from the purest malice on the part of the suicide.

Their majesties the mob, with that beautiful consistency which usually distinguishes those august individuals, insisted upon shooting poor Harry—for said they, and the reasoning is remarkably conclusive and clear, "a man so hardened as to raise his hand against his *own* life, will never hesitate to murder another!" They almost mobbed F. for binding up the wounds of the unfortunate wretch and for saying that it was possible he might live. At last, however, they compromised the matter, by determining, that if Henry should recover, he should leave the Bar immediately. Neither contingency will probably take place, as it will be almost a miracle if he survives.

On the day following the attempted suicide, which was Sunday, nothing more exciting happened than a fight and the half-drowning of a drunken individual in the river, just in front of the Humboldt.

On Sunday last, the thigh of Señor Pizarro was amputated; but alas, without success. He had been sick for many months with chronic dysentery, which after the operation returned with great violence, and he died at two o'clock on Monday morning with the same calm and lofty resignation which had distinguished him during his illness. When first wounded, believing his case hopeless, he had deci-

dedly refused to submit to amputation, but as time wore
on he was persuaded to take this one chance for his life,
for the sake of his daughter, a young girl of fifteen, at present at school in a convent in Chili, whom his death leaves
without any near relation. I saw him several times during
his illness, and it was melancholy indeed, to hear him talk
of his motherless girl who, I have been told, is extremely
beautiful, talented and accomplished.

The state of society here has never been so bad as since
the appointment of a Committee of Vigilance. The rowdies have formed themselves into a company called the
"Moguls," and they parade the streets all night, howling,
shouting, breaking into houses, taking wearied miners out
of their beds and throwing them into the river, and in
short, "murdering sleep," in the most remorseless manner. Nearly every night they build bonfires fearfully near
some rag shanty, thus endangering the lives, (or I should
rather say the property—for as it is impossible to sleep,
lives are emphatically safe) of the whole community.
They retire about five o'clock in the morning; previously
to this blessed event posting notices to that effect, and
that they will throw any one who may disturb them into
the river. I am nearly worn out for want of rest, for truly
they "make night hideous" with their fearful uproar. Mr.
O———, who still lies dangerously ill from the wound received, on what we call the "fatal Sunday," complains bit-
terly of the disturbance; and when poor Pizarro was dying, and one of his friends gently requested that they
would be quiet for half an hour and permit the soul of the
sufferer to pass in peace, they only laughed and yelled and
hooted louder than ever, in the presence of the departing
spirit, for the tenement in which he lay, being composed
of green boughs only, could of course shut out no sounds.
Without doubt if the "Moguls" had been sober, they

would never have been guilty of such horrible barbarity as
to compel the thoughts of a dying man to mingle with
curses and blasphemies; but alas! they were intoxicated,
and may God forgive them, unhappy ones, for they knew
not what they did. The poor, exhausted miners, for even
well people cannot sleep in such a pandemonium, grumble
and complain, but they—although far outnumbering the
rioters—are too timid to resist. All say "It is shameful;
something ought to be done; something *must* be done,"
etc. and in the mean time the rioters triumph. You will
wonder that the Committee of Vigilance does not interfere; it is said that some of that very Committee are the
ringleaders among the "Moguls."

I believe I have related to you everything but the duel—
and I will make the recital of this as short as possible, for I
am sick of these sad subjects, and doubt not but you are
the same. It took place on Tuesday morning at eight
o'clock, on Missouri Bar, when and where that same Englishman who has figured so largely in my letter, shot his
best friend. The duelists were surrounded by a large
crowd, I have been told, foremost among which stood the
Committee of Vigilance! The man who received his dear
friend's fatal shot, was one of the most quiet and peace-
able citizens on the Bar. He lived about ten minutes after
he was wounded. He was from Ipswich, England, and only
twenty-five years of age, when his own high passions
snatched him from life. In justice to his opponent, it must
be said, that he would willingly have retired after the first
shots had been exchanged, but poor Billy Leggett, as he
was familiarly called, insisted upon having the distance between them shortened, and continuing the duel until one
of them had fallen.

There, my dear M., have I not fulfilled my promise of
giving you a dish of horrors? And only think of such a

shrinking, timid, frail thing, as I *used* to be "long time ago," not only living right in the midst of them, but almost compelled to hear if not see the whole. I think that I may without vanity affirm, that I have "seen the elephant." "Did you see his tail?" asks innocent Ada J., in her mother's letter. Yes, sweet Ada, the "entire Animal" has been exhibited to my view. "But you must remember, that this is California," as the new comers are so fond of informing *us*! who consider ourselves "one of the oldest inhabitants" of the golden State.

And now dear M., *A Dios*. Be thankful that you are living in the beautiful quiet of beautiful A., and give up "hankering arter" (as you know what dear creature says—) California, for believe me, this coarse, barbarous life would suit you, even less than it does your sister.

LETTER TWENTIETH

From our Log Cabin, Indïan Bar,
Sept. 4, 1852

IF I could coax some good-natured fairy, or some mischievous Puck, to borrow for me the pen of Grace Greenwood, Fanny Forester, or Nathaniel Willis, I might be able to weave my stupid nothings into one of those airy fabrics, the value of which depends entirely upon the skillful work—or, rather penmanship—which distinguishes it. I have even fancied, that if I could steal a feather from the living opal, swinging like a jeweled pendulum from the heart of the great tiger-lily, which nods its turbaned head so stately within the mosquito net-cage standing upon the little table—my poor lines would gather a certain beauty from the rainbow-tinted quill, with which I might trace them. But as there is nobody magician enough, to go out and shoot a fairy or a brownie, and bind it by sign and spell to do my bidding, and as I have strong doubts whether my coarse fingers would be able to manage the delicate pen of a humming-bird, even if I could have the heart to rob my only remaining pet of its brilliant feathers, I am fain to be content with one of "Gillott's Best," no; of "C.R. Sheton's Extra Fine," although certain that the sentences following its hard-stroke will be as stiff as itself. If they were only as bright, one might put up with the want of grace; but, to be stiff and stupid both, is *too* provoking, is it not, Dear M.? However, what must be, must be; and as I have nothing to write about, and do not possess the skill to make that nothing graceful, and as you

will fret yourself into a scold if you do not receive the
usual amount of inked pages at the usual time—why, of
course, I am bound to act (my first appearance on *any*
stage, I flatter myself in *that* character—) the very original
part of the *bore*, and you must prepare to be bored with
what philosophy you may.

But without further preface, I will begin with one of
the nothings. A few days after the death of the unfortunate Spaniard, related in my last letter, a large log, felled by
some wickedly-careless woodman, rolled down from one
of the hills, and so completely extinguished the little
Ramara, in which our poor friend lay at the time of his
death, that you would never have imagined from the heap
of broken branches which remain, that it had once been a
"local habitation," with such a pretty "name." Provi-
dentially, at the time of the accident, none of those who
had been in the habit of stopping there, were within. If
Señor Pizarro had survived the amputation of his leg, it
would only have been to suffer a still more terrible death,
—an accident, which would have deepened, if possible, the
gloom which we have suffered during the melancholy
summer.

There has been another murder committed within a
few miles of this place, which has given us something to
gossip about; for the Committee of Vigilance had the
good-nature, purely for our amusement I conclude, to ap-
prehend a lucky individual, (I call him *lucky* advisedly; for
he had all his expenses paid at the Humboldt—was remun-
erated for his lost time—enjoyed a holiday from hard
work—had a sort of guard-of-honor, composed of the
most respectable men on the River—and was of more consequence for four days, than ever he had been in the whole
of his insignificant little life before;) whom somebody
fancied bore a faint resemblance to the description of the

murderer. This interesting lion—I was so fortunate as to catch a glimpse of him one morning, and am convinced that he "would have roared you like any sucking dove," was fully cleared from the suspected crime; and if before his acquittal, one might have fancied from the descriptions of his countenance, that none but that of Mephistopheles, in the celebrated picture of the Game of Life, could equal its terrific malignity, after accounts drew it a very St. John's, for sweet serenity of expression; what was then called sullenness, now took the name of resignation, and stupidity was quiet contempt. Indeed, I began to fear that they would give him a public triumph, and invite me to make the flag with which to grace it. I confess that I would almost have voted him a procession myself, in gratitude for the amusement which he had given us. However, the Committee were contented with making him a handsome apology and present, and paying his expenses at the Humboldt. Oh, public opinion in the Mines, thou are in truth a *cruel* thing, but at the same time, thank God, most *fickle*!

The other day, we were invited by a Spanish friend to breakfast, at a garden situated half a mile from the Junction, and owned by another Spaniard. It was a lovely morning, in the latter part of August, and as we started about six o'clock, the walk was a most delightful one. The River, filled with flumes, dams, etc., and crowded with busy miners, was as much altered from its old appearance, as if an earthquake had frightened it from its propriety.

I suppose that you are quite worn out with descriptions of walks, and I will spare you this once. I will not tell you, how sometimes we were stepping lightly over immense rocks, which a few months since, lay fathoms deep beneath the foaming Plumas; nor how sometimes we were walking high above the bed of the river, from flume to

flume, across a board, connecting the two; nor, how now
we were scrambling over the roots of the up-turned trees,
and now jumping tiny rivulets; nor shall I say a single word
about the dizziness we felt, as we crept by the deep excavations lying along the road, nor of the beautiful walk at
the side of the wing-dam, (it differs from a common dam,
in dividing the river lengthways instead of across,) the glittering water rising bluely, almost to a level with the path. I
do not think that I will ever tell you about the *impromptu*
bath which one of the party took, by tumbling accidentally into the river, as he was walking gallantly behind
us; which, said bath, made him decidedly disagree in our
enthusiastic opinion of the loveliness of the promenade.

No; I shall not say a single word upon any of these subjects, but leave them all to your vivid imagination. Cork-
-screws could not draw a solitary sentence from me, now
that I have made up my mind to silence. But, I *will* tell you
about the "driftings" in the side of the hill, which we
visited on our way—not so much from a precious desire of
enlightening your pitiable ignorance upon such subjects,
you poor little, untraveled Yankee woman! but to prove
to you, that having fathomed the depths of "shafts," and
threaded the mazes of "Coyote Holes," I intend to astonish the weak nerves of stay-at-homes—if I ever return to
New England—by talking learnedly on such subjects, as
"one having authority."

These particular "claims," consist of three galleries, lying about eighty feet beneath the summit of the hill, and
have already been "drifted" from one hundred and fifty
to two hundred feet into its side. They are about five feet
in height, slightly arched, the sides and roof formed of
rugged rocks, dripping with moisture as if sweating beneath the great weight above. Lights are placed at regular
distances along these galleries to assist the miners in their

work, and boards laid on the wet ground to make a convenient path for the wheelbarrows which convey the dirt
and sand to the river, for the purpose of washing it.
Wooden beams are placed here and there, to lessen the
danger of caving in; but I must confess, that in spite of this
precaution, I was first haunted with a horrible feeling of
insecurity. As I became reassured, I repeated loudly those
glorious lines of Mrs. Hemans, commencing with—

> "For the strength of the hills, we bless thee;
> Our God, our Fathers' God!"

And a strange echo the gray rocks sent back; as if the
mine-demons, those ugly gnomes, which German legends
tell us, work forever in the bowels of the earth, were
shouting my words in mockery from the dim depths beyond.

These "claims" have paid remarkably well, and if they
hold out as they have commenced, the owners will gather
a small fortune from their Summer's work.

There is nothing which impresses me more strangely
than the fluming operations. The idea of a mighty river
being taken up in a wooden trough, turned from the old
channel, along which it has foamed for centuries, perhaps,
its bed excavated many feet in depth, and itself restored
to its old home in the fall, these things strike me as almost
a blasphemy against Nature. And then the idea of men
succeeding in such a work, here in the mountains, with
machinery and tools of the poorest description, to say
nothing of the unskillful workmen, doctors, lawyers,
ministers, scholars, gentlemen, farmers, etc.

When we arrived at the little oak opening described in a
former letter, we were, of course, in duty bound to take a
draught from the spring, which its admirers declare, is the

best water in all California. When it came to my turn, I
complacently touched the rusty tin cup, though I never
did care much for water in the abstract *as* water; though I
think it very useful to make coffee, tea, chocolate, and
other good drinks, I could never detect any other flavor in
it than that of *cold*, and have often wondered whether
there was any truth in the remark of a character in some
play, "that ever since the world was drowned in it, it had
tasted of sinners!"

When we arrived at—what may be called in reference to
the Bar—the country seat of Don Juan, we were ushered
into the parlor, two sides of which opened upon the garden, and the grand old mountains which rise behind it,
while the other two sides and the roof were woven with
fresh willow boughs, crisply green, and looking as if the
dew had scarcely yet dried from the polished leaves.

After opening some cans of peaches, and cutting up
some watermelons gathered from the garden, our friends
went into, or rather *out* to the kitchen fire (two or three
stones is generally the extent of this useful apartment in
the mines), to assist in preparing the breakfast—and *such* a
breakfast! If "Tadger could do it when it chose," so can
we miners. We had—but what did we *not* have? There were
oysters, which, I am sure, could not have been nicer had
they just slid from their shells on the shore at Amboy;
salmon, in color like the "red, red gold"; venison, with a
fragrant, spicy gusto, as if it had been fed on cedar buds;
beef cooked in the Spanish fashion—that is, strung on to a
skewer, and roasted on the coals—than which, I never
tasted better; preserved chicken, and almost every possible vegetable bringing up the rear. Then, for drinkables,
we had tea, coffee and chocolate, champagne, claret and
porter, with stronger spirits *for* the stronger spirits. We
lacked but one thing, that was ice, which we forgot to

bring from the Bar—as only four miles from our cabin, the snow never melts, that is a luxury we are never without— and, indeed, so excessively warm has been the season, that without it, and the milk which has been brought us daily from a ranch five miles from here, we should have suffered. I must say, that even though we had no ice, our mountain pic-nic, with its attendant dandies, in their blue and red flannel shirts, was the most charming affair of the kind that I ever attended.

On our return, we called to see "Yank's" cub, which is fast rising into young grizzly-bear-hood. It is about the size of a calf, very good-natured, and quite tame. Its acquirements, as yet, are few, being limited to climbing a pole. Its education has not been conducted with that care and attention which so intelligent a beast merits, but it is soon, I hear, to be removed to the valley, and placed under teachers capable of developing its wonderful talents to the utmost.

We also stopped at a shanty to get a large gray squirrel, which had been promised to me some days' before; but I certainly am the most unfortunate wretch in the world with pets. This spiteful thing, on purpose to annoy me, I do believe, went and got itself drowned the very night before I was to take it home. It is always so—

> I never had two humming-birds,
>   With plumage like a sunset sky,
> But one was sure to fly away,
>   And the other one was sure to die.
>
> I never nursed a flying squirrel,
>   To glad me with its soft black eye,
> But it always ran into somebody's tent,
>   Got mistaken for a rat and killed!

There, M., there is poetry for you. "Oh, the second verse doesn't rhyme." "Doesn't?" "And it ain't original, isn't it?" Well, *I* never heard that rhyme was necessary to make a poet, any more than colors to make a painter. And what if Moore *did* say the same thing twenty years ago? I am sure any writer would consider himself lucky to have an idea which has been anticipated but *once*. I am tired of being a "mute inglorious Milton," and like that grand old master of English song, would gladly write "something which the world would not willingly let die," and having made the first step, as witness the above verses, who knows what will follow.

Last night, one of our neighbors had a dinner party. He came in to borrow a teaspoon. "Had you not better take them all?" I said. "Oh, no," was the answer, "that would be too much luxury. My guests are not used to it, and they would think that I was getting aristocratic, and putting on airs. One is enough; they can pass it round from one to the other."

A blacksmith—not the "learned" one—has just entered, inquiring for the doctor, who is not in, and he is obliged to wait. Shall I write down the conversation with which he is at this moment entertaining me? "Who writ this 'ere?" is his first remark, taking up one of my most precious books, and leaving the marks of his irreverent fingers upon the clean pages. "Shakespeare," I answer, as politely as possible. "Did Spokshave write it? He was an almighty smart fellow, that Spokshave, I've hear'n tell," replies my visitor. "I must write hum, and tell our folks that this 'ere is the first carpet I've seen sin I came to Californy, four year come next month," is his next remark. For the last half-hour, he has been entertaining me with a wearisome account of the murder of his brother by an Irishman, in Boston, and the chief feeling which he exhibits, is a fear that the jury should only bring a verdict of manslaughter. But I hear F.'s step and his entrance relieves me from the bore.

I am too tired to write more. Alas, dear M., this letter is indeed a stupid one—a poor return for your pregnant epistles. It is too late to better it; the express goes at eight in the morning. The midnight moon is looking wonderingly in at the cabin window, and the river has a sleepy murmur, that impels me irresistibly bedward.

RESIDENCE IN THE MINES

From our Log Cabin, Indian Bar,
Oct. 16 1852

SINCE I last wrote you, dear M., I have spent three weeks in the American Valley, and I returned therefrom humbled to the very dust, when thinking of my former vainglorious boast of having "seen the elephant." To be sure, if having fathomed to its very depths the power of mere existence, without any reference to those conventional aids which civilization has the folly to think necessary to the performance of that agreeable duty, was any criterion, I certainly fancied that I had a right to brag of having taken a full view of that most piquant specimen of the brute creation, the California "Elephant." But it seems that I was mistaken, and that we miners have been dwelling in perfect palaces, surrounded by furniture of the most gorgeous description, and reveling in every possible luxury. Well, one lives and learns, even on the borders of civilization. But to begin at the beginning, let me tell you the history of my dreadful pleasure tour to the American Valley.

You must know that a convention had been appointed to meet at that place, for the purpose of nominating representatives for the coming election. As F. had the misfortune to be one of the delegates, nothing would do but I must accompany him; for as my health had really suffered through the excitements of the summer, he fancied that change of air might do me good. Mrs. ——, one of our new ladies, had been invited to spend a few weeks in the same place, at the residence of a friend of her husband, who was living there with his family. As Mr. —— was also one of the delegates, we made up a party together, and being joined by two or three other gentlemen, formed quite a gay cavalcade.

The day was beautiful; but when is it ever otherwise in the mountains of California? We left the Bar by another ascent than the one from which I entered the Bar, and it was so infinitely less steep than the latter, that it seemed a mere nothing. You, however, would have fancied it quite a respectable hill, and Mr. —— said, that so fearful did it seem to him the first time he went down it, that he vowed never to cross it but once more; a vow, by the way, which has been broken many times. The whole road was a succession of charming tableaux, in which sparkling streamlets, tiny waterfalls, frisky squirrels gleaming amid the foliage like a flash of red light; quails, with their pretty gray plumage flecked with ivory; dandy jays, great awkward black crows, pert little lizards, innumerable butterflies, and a hundred other

> "Plumed insects, winged and free,
> Like golden boats on a sunny sea,"

were the characters, grouped in a frame of living green, curtained with the blue folds of our inimitable sky.

We had intended to start very early in the morning, but, as usual on such excursions, did not get off until about ten o'clock. Somebody's horse came up missing, or somebody's saddle needed repairing, or somebody's shirt did not come home in season from the washer-Chinaman—for if we *do* wear flannel shirts, we choose to have them clean when we ride out with the ladies—or something else equally important detained us. It was about nine o'clock in the evening when we reached the valley, and rode up to Greenwood's Rancho, which, by the way, was the headquarters of the Democratic party. It was crowded to overflowing, as our ears told us, long before we came in sight of it, and we found it utterly impossible to obtain lodgings there. This building has no windows, but a strip of crimson calico, placed half-way from the roof and running all round the house, lets in the *red* light and supplies their place. However, we did not stop long to enjoy the pictorial effect of the scarlet windows—which really look very prettily in the night—but rode straight to the American Rancho, a quarter of a mile beyond. This was the headquarters of the Whigs, to which party our entire company, excepting myself, belonged. Indeed, the gentlemen had only consented to call at the other house through compassion for the ladies, who were suffering from extreme fatigue, and they were rejoiced at the prospect of getting among birds of the same feather. There, however, we were informed that it was equally impossible to procure accommodations. In this dilemma, we could do nothing but accept Mrs. ——'s kind invitation, and accompany her to the rancho of her friend, although she herself had intended, as it was so late, to stop at one of the hotels for the night. We were so lucky as to procure a guide at this place, and with this desirable addition to the party, we started on.

I had been very sick for the last two hours, and had only kept up with the thought that we should soon arrive at our journey's end; but when I found that we were compelled to ride three miles further, my heart sank within me; I gave up all attempts to guide my horse, which one of the party led, leaned my head on the horn of my saddle and resigned myself to my fate. We were obliged to walk our horses the entire distance, as I was too sick to endure any other motion. We lost our way once or twice; were exhausted with fatigue and faint with hunger, chilled through with the cold and our feet wet with the damp night air.

I forgot to tell you that Mrs. ——, being very fleshy, was compelled to ride astride, as it would have been utterly impossible for her to have kept her seat if she had attempted to cross those steep hills in the usual feminine mode of sitting a horse. She wore dark gray bloomers, and with a Kossuth hat and feather, looked like a handsome, chubby boy. Now, riding astride, to one unaccustomed to it, is, as you can easily imagine, more safe than comfortable, and poor Mrs. —— was utterly exhausted.

When we arrived at our destined haven, which we did at last, the gentleman of the house came forward and invited Mr. and Mrs. —— to alight. Not a word was said to the rest of us, not even "Good evening;" but I was too far gone to stand upon ceremony, so I dismounted and made a rush for the cooking-stove, which, in company with an immense dining table, on which lay (enchanting sight) a quarter of beef, stood under a roof, the four sides open to the winds of heaven. As for the remainder of the party, they saw how the land lay, and *vamosed* to parts unknown, (namely the American Rancho,) where they arrived at four o'clock in the morning, some tired, I *guess*, and made such a fearful inroad upon the eatables, that the proprietor stood aghast, and was only pacified by the ordering in from the bar, of a most generous supply of the drinkable, which, as he sells it by the glass, somewhat reconciled him to the terrific onslaught upon the larder.

In the mean time, behold me, with much more truth than poetry, literally "alone in my glory," seated upon a wooden stool, with both feet perched upon the stove, and crouching over the fire in a vain attempt to coax some warmth into my thoroughly chilled frame. The gentleman and lady of the house, with Mr. and Mrs. ——, are assembled in grand conclave, in one room of which the building consists; and as California houses are *not* planned with a view to eavesdroppers, I have the pleasure of hearing the following spirited and highly interesting conversation. There is a touching simplicity about it truly dramatic:

I must premise, that Mrs. —— had written the day before, to know if the visit, which her husband's friend had so earnestly solicited, would be conveniently received at this time; and was answered by the arrival the next morning, for the use of herself and husband, of two horses, one of which, I myself had the pleasure of riding, and found it a most excellent steed. Moreover, when Mr. —— gave her the invitation, he said he would be pleased to have one of her lady friends accompany her. So you see she was "armed and equipped as the law directed."

Thus defended, she was ushered into the presence of her hostess, whom she found reclining gracefully upon a very nice bed, hung with snow-white muslin curtains, looking—for she is extremely pretty, though now somewhat pale—like a handsome wax doll.

"I am extremely sorry to find you unwell. Pray, when were you taken, and are you suffering much at present?" commenced Mrs. —— supposing that her illness was merely an attack of headache or some other temporary sickness.

"Ah," groaned my lady in a faint voice, "I have had a fever and am just beginning to get a little better. I have not been able to sit up any yet, but hope to do so in a few days. As we have no servants, my husband is obliged to nurse me as well as to cook for several men, and I am really afraid that under the circumstances, you will not be as comfortable here as I could wish."

"But, good heavens, my dear madam, why did you not send me word that you were sick? Surely you must have known that it would be more agreeable to me to visit you when you are in health?" replied Mrs. ——.

"Oh," returned our fair invalid, "I thought that you had set your heart upon coming, and would be disappointed if I postponed the visit!"

Now this was adding insult to injury. Poor Mrs. ——! worn out with hunger, shivering with cold, herself far from well, a new comer, unused to the make-shift ways which some people fancy essential to California life, expecting from the husband's representations, and knowing that he was very rich, so different a reception; and withal, frank perhaps to a fault, she must be pardoned if she was not as grateful as she ought to have been, and answered a little crossly:

"Well, I must say, that I have not been treated well. Did you really think that I was so childishly crazy to get away from home, that I would leave my nice plank house," (it rose into palatial splendor, when compared with the floorless shanty, less comfortable than a Yankee farmer's barn, in which she was standing,) "with its noble fireplace, nice board floor, two pleasant windows and comfortable bed, for this wretched place? Upon my word, I am very much disappointed. However, I do not care so much for myself as for poor Mrs. ——, whom I persuaded to come with me."

"What, is there *another* lady!" almost shrieked (and well she might under the circumstances) the horror-stricken hostess. "You can sleep with me, but I am sure I do not know what we can do with another one."

"Certainly," was the bold reply of Mrs. ——, for she was too much provoked to be embarrassed in the least; "availing myself of your husband's kind permission, I invited Mrs. ——, who could not procure lodgings at either of the hotels, to accompany me. But even if I were alone, I should decidedly object to sleep with a sick person, and should infinitely prefer wrapping myself in my shawl and lying on the ground, to being guilty of such a piece of selfishness."

"Well," groaned the poor woman, "Jonathan," or Ichabod, or David, or whatever was the domestic name of her better half, "I suppose that you must make up some kind of a bed for them on the ground."

Now M., only fancy my hearing all this! *Wasn't* it a fix for a sensitive person to be in? But instead of bursting into tears, and making myself miserable, as once I should have done, I enjoyed the *contra temps* immensely. It almost cured my headache, and when Mrs. —— came to me and tried to soften matters, I told her to spare her pretty speeches, as I had heard the whole and would not have missed it for anything.

In the mean time, the useful little man, combining in his small person the four functions of husband, cook, nurse and gentleman, made us a cup of tea and some saleratus biscuit; and though I detest saleratus biscuit, and was longing for some of the beef; yet by killing the taste of the alkali with onions, we contrived to satisfy our hunger, and the tea warmed us a little. Our host, in his capacity of chambermaid, had prepared us a couch. I was ushered into the presence of the fair invalid, to whom I made a polite apology for my intrusion. My feet sank nearly to the ankles in the dirt and small stones as I walked across her room.

But how shall I describe to you the sufferings of that dreadful night? I have slept on tables, on doors, and on trunks; I have reclined on couches, on chairs, and on the floor; I have lain on beds of straw, of corn-husks, of palm-leaf, and of ox-hide; I remember one awful night, spent in a bed-buggy berth, on board of a packet boat on one of the lakes; in my younger days, I used to allow myself to be stretched upon the Procrustes bed of other people's opin-ion, though I have got bravely over such folly, and now I generally act, think and speak as best pleases myself; I slept two glorious nights on the bare turf, with my saddle for a pillow and God's kindly sky for a quilt; I had *heard* of a bed of thorns, of the soft side of a plank, and of the "bed-rock"; but all my *bodily* experience, theoretical or practical, sinks into insignificance before a bed of cobble-stones! Nothing in ancient or modern history, can com-pare with it, unless it be the Irishman's famous down-couch, which consisted of a single feather laid upon a rock; and like him, if it had not been for the name of it, I should have preferred the bare rock. They *said* that there was straw in the ticking upon which we lay, but I should never have imagined so from the feeling. We had neither pillows nor sheets, but the coarsest blue blankets, and not enough of them, for bed-clothes; so that we suffered with cold, to add to our other miseries. And then, the fleas! Well, like the Grecian artist, who veiled the face whose anguish he dared not attempt to depict, I will leave to your imagination, that blackest portion of our strange experiences on that awful occasion.

What became of Mr. ——, our host, etc., on this dreadful night, was never known. Mrs. —— and I, held council to-gether, and concluded that he was spirited away to some friendly hay-stack; but as he himself maintained a pro-found silence on the subject, it remains to this hour an impenetrable mystery, and will be handed down to pos-

terity on the page of history, with that of the "Man in the
Iron Mask," and the more modern, but equally unsolvable
riddle, of "Who struck Billy Patterson?"

As soon as it was light, we awoke and glanced around
the room. On one side, hung a large quantity of handsome
dresses, with a riding habit, hat, gauntlets, whip, saddle
and bridle, all of the most elegant description. On the
other side, a row of shelves contained a number of pans of
milk. There was also a very pretty table service of white
crockery, a roll of white carpeting, boxes of soap, chests
of tea, casks of sugar, bags of coffee, etc., etc., in the greatest profusion.

We went out into the air. The place, owned by our host,
is the most beautiful spot that I ever saw in California. We
stood in the midst of a noble grove of the loftiest and
largest trees, through which ran two or three carriage
roads, with not a particle of undergrowth to be seen in any
direction. Somewhere near the center of this lovely place,
he is building a house of hewn logs. It will be two stories
high and very large. He intends finishing it with the piazza
all around, the first floor windows to the ground, green
blinds, etc. He informed us that he thought it would be
finished in three weeks. You can see that it would have
been much pleasanter for Mrs. —— to have had the privi-
lege of deferring her visit for a month.

We had a most excellent breakfast. As Mrs. —— said, the
good people possessed everything but a house.

Soon after breakfast, my friends, who suspected from
appearances the night before that I should not prove a
very welcome visitor, came for me—the wife of the proprietor of the American Rancho having good-naturedly retired to the privacy of a covered-wagon, (she had just
crossed the plains,) and placed her own room at my dis-

posal. Mrs. —— insisted upon accompanying me until her friend was better. As she truly said, she was too unwell herself, to either assist or amuse another invalid.

My apartment, which was built of logs, was vexatiously small, with no way of letting in light, except by the door. It was as innocent of a floor, and almost as thickly strewn with cobble-stones, as the one which I had just left; but then there *were* some frames built against the side of it, which served for a bed-stead, and we had sheets, which though coarse, were clean. Here, with petticoats, stockings, shoes and shirts, hanging against the logs in picturesque confusion, we received calls from Senators, Representatives, Judges, Attorney-Generals, Doctors, Lawyers, Officers, Editors and Ministers.

The Convention came off the day after our arrival in the valley; and as both of the nominees were from our settlement, we began to think that we were quite a people.

Horse-racing, and gambling, in all their detestable varieties, were the order of the day. There was faro and poker for the Americans, monte for the Spaniards, lansquenet for the Frenchmen, and smaller games for the "outsiders."

At the close of the Convention, the rancho passed into new hands, and as there was much consequent confusion, I went over to Greenwoods, and Mrs. —— returned to the house of her friend, where, having ordered two or three hundred armfuls of hay to be strewn on the ground, she made a "temporary arrangement" with some boards for a bedstead, and fell to making sheets from one of the innumerable rolls of cloth which lay about in every direction; for as I said before, these good people had everything but a house.

My new room, with the exception of its red calico window, was exactly like the old one. Although it was very small, a man and his wife—the latter was the housekeeper of the establishment—slept there also. With the aid of those everlasting blue blankets, I curtained off our part, so as to obtain some small degree of privacy. I had *one* large pocket handkerchief—it was meant for a young sheet—on my bed, which was filled with good, sweet, fresh hay, and plenty of the azure coverings, so short and narrow, that when once we had lain down, it behooved us to remain perfectly still until morning, as the least movement dis-arranged the bed furniture and insured us a shivering night.

On the other side of the partition, against which our bedstead was *built*, stood the cooking-stove, in which they burnt nothing but pitch-pine wood. As the room was not lined, and the boards very loosely put together, the soot sifted through in large quantities, and covered us from head to foot, and though I bathed so often that my hands were dreadfully chapped and bled profusely, from having them so much in the water, yet in spite of my ef-forts, I looked like a chimney-sweep, masquerading in women's clothes.

As it was very cold at this time, the damp ground upon which we were living, gave me a severe cough, and I suf-fered so much from chillness that at last I betook myself to Rob Roy shawls and India rubbers, and for the rest of the time walked about, a mere bundle of gum elastic and Scotch plaid. My first move in the morning, was to go out and sit upon an old traveling wagon, which stood in front of my room, in order, like an old beggar woman, to gather a little warmth from the sun.

Mrs. —— said, "The Bostonians were horror-stricken, because the poor Irish—who had never known any other mode of living—had no floors in their cabins, and were get-ting up all sorts of 'Howard Benevolent Societies,' to supply unfortunate Pat with what is to him an unwished for luxury." She thought, "That they would be much better employed in organizing associations for ameliorating the conditions of those wretched women in California, who were so mad as to leave their comfortable homes in the mines, to go a pleasuring in the valleys!"

My poor husband suffered even more than I did, for though he had a nominal share in my luxurious bed with its accompanying pocket handkerchief, yet, as Mrs. —— took it into her head to pay me a visit, he was obliged to resign it to her and betake himself to the bar-room; and as every bunk and all the blankets were engaged, he was com-pelled to lie on the bar floor, (thank Heaven there was a civilized floor there of real boards,) with his boots for a pillow.

But I am sure you must be tired of this long letter, for I am, and I reserve the rest of my adventures in the Ameri-can Valley, until another time.

LETTER TWENTY-SECOND

RESIDENCE IN THE MINES

From our Log Cabin, Indian Bar,
Oct. 27, 1852

IN MY last epistle, my dear M., I left myself safely ensconced at Greenwood's Rancho, in about as uncomfortable a position as a person could well be, where board was fourteen dollars a week. Now you must not think that the proprietors were at all to blame for our miserable condition. They were, I assure you, very gentlemanly and intelligent men; and I owe them a thousand thanks, for the many acts of kindness, and the friendly efforts which they made to amuse and interest me while I was in their house. They said from the first that they were utterly unprepared to receive ladies, and it was only after some persuasion, and as a favor to me, that they consented to let me come. They intend soon to build a handsome house; for it is thought that this valley will be a favorite summer resort for people from the cities below.

The American Valley is one of the most beautiful in all California. It is seven miles long and three or four wide, with the Feather River wending its quiet way through it, unmolested by flumes, and undisturbed by wing dams. It is a superb farming country, everything growing in the greatest luxuriance. I saw turnips there which measured larger round than my waist, and all other vegetables in the same proportion. There are beautiful rides in every direction; though I was too unwell during my stay there to explore them as I wished. There is one draw-back upon the beauty of these valleys, and it is one peculiar to all the

scenery in this part of California—and that is, the monotonous tone of the foliage, nearly all the trees being firs.
One misses that infinite variety of waving forms, and
those endless shades of verdure, which make New England
forest scenery so exquisitely lovely. And then that gorgeous autumnal phenomenon, witnessed, I believe, nowhere but in the Northern States of the Union, one never
sees here. How often, in my far-away Yankee home, have I
laid me down at eve, with the whole earth looking so
freshly green, to rise in the morning and behold the wilderness blossoming, not only like the rose, but like all
other flowers beside, and glittering as if a shower of butterflies had fallen upon it during the silent watches of the
night. I have a vague idea that I "hooked" that butterfly
comparison from somebody. If so, I beg the injured person's pardon, and he or she may have a hundred of *mine* to
pay for it.

It was at Greenwood's Rancho, that the famous quartz
hoax originated last winter, which so completely gulled
our good miners on the river. I visited the spot, which has
been excavated to some extent. The stone is very beautiful, being lined and streaked and splashed with crimson,
purple, green, orange, and black. There was one large
white block, veined with stripes of a magnificent blood-
red color, and partly covered with a dark mass, which was
the handsomest thing of the kind I ever saw. Some of the
crystallizations were wonderfully perfect. I had a piece of
the bed rock given me, completely covered with natural
prisms, varying in size from an inch down to those not
larger than the head of a pin.

Much of the immigration from across the plains, on its
way to the cities below, stops here for awhile to recruit. I
always had a strange fancy for that Nomadic way of coming to California. To lie down under starry skies, hundreds

of miles from any human habitation, and to rise up on dewy mornings, to pursue our way through a strange country, so wildly beautiful, seeing each day something new and wonderful, seemed to me truly enchanting. But cruel reality strips *everything* of its rose tints. The poor women arrive, looking as haggard as so many Endorean witches; burnt to the color of a hazel-nut, with their hair cut short, and its gloss entirely destroyed by the alkali, whole plains of which they are compelled to cross on the way. You will hardly find a family that has not left some beloved one buried upon the plains. And they are fearful funerals, those. A person dies, and they stop just long enough to dig his grave and lay him in it, as decently as circumstances will permit, and the long train hurries on-ward, leaving its healthy companion of yesterday, per-haps, in this boundless city of the dead. On this hazardous journey, they dare not linger.

I was acquainted with a young widow of twenty, whose husband died of cholera when they were but five weeks on their journey. He was a Judge in one of the Western States, and a man of some eminence in his profession. She is a pretty little creature, and all the aspirants to matrimony are candidates for her hand.

One day a party of immigrant women came into my room, which was also the parlor of the establishment. Some observation was made, which led me to enquire of one of them if her husband was with her.

"She hain't got no husband," fairly *chuckled* one of her companions; "She came with *me*, and her feller died of cholera on the plains!"

At this startling and brutal announcement, the poor girl herself gave a hysteric giggle, which I at first thought pro-ceeded from heartlessness; but I was told afterwards, by the person under whose immediate protection she came out, and who was a sister of her betrothed, that the tender woman's heart received such a fearful shock at the sudden death of her lover, that for several weeks her life was despaired of.

I spent a great deal of time calling at the different encampments; for nothing enchanted me half so much as to hear about this strange exodus from the States. I never weary of listening to stories of adventures on the plains, and some of the family histories are deeply interesting.

I was acquainted with four women, all sisters or sisters-in-law, who had among them thirty-six children, the entire number of which had arrived thus far in perfect health. They could of themselves form quite a respectable village.

The immigration this year, contained many intelligent and truly elegant persons, who, having caught the fashionable epidemic, had left luxurious homes in the States, to come to California. Among others, there was a young gentleman of nineteen, the son of a United States Senator, who having just graduated, felt adventurous, and determined to cross the plains. Like the rest, he arrived in a somewhat dilapidated condition, with elbows out, and a hat the very counterpart of Sam Weller's "gossamer ventilation," which, if you remember, "though *not* a very hansome 'un to look at, was an astonishin' good 'un to wear!" I must confess that he became ragged clothes the best of any one I ever saw, and made me think of the picturesque beggar boys, in Murillo's paintings of Spanish life.

Then there was a person, who used to sing in public with Ossian Dodge. He had a voice of remarkable purity and sweetness, which he was kind enough to permit us to hear now and then. I hardly know of what nation he claimed to be. His father was an Englishman, his mother an Italian; he was born in Poland, and had lived nearly all

his life in the United States. He was not the only musical
genius that we had among us. There was a little girl at one
of the tents, who had taught herself to play on the accor-
dion on the way out. She was really quite a prodigy, singing very sweetly, and accompanying herself with much
skill upon the instrument.

There was another child, whom I used to go to look at,
as I would go to examine a picture. She had, without exception, the most beautiful face I ever saw. Even the alkali
had not been able to mar the golden glory of the curls
which clustered around that splendid little head. She had
soft brown eyes, which shone from beneath their silken
lashes, like "a tremulous evening star;" a mouth which
made you think of a string of pearls threaded on scarlet;
and a complexion of the waxen purity of the japonica,
with the exception of a band of brownest freckles, which,
extending from the tip of each cheek straight across the
prettiest possible nose, added, I used to fancy, a new
beauty to her enchanting face. She was very fond of me,
and used to bring me wild cherries which her brothers had
gathered for her. Many a morning I have raised my eyes
from my book, startled by that vision of infant loveliness
—for her step had the still grace of a snow-flake—standing
in beautiful silence by my side.

But the most interesting of all my pets was a widow,
whom we used to call the "long woman." When but a few
weeks on the journey, she had buried her husband, who
died of cholera after about six hours illness. She had come
on; for what else could she do? No one was willing to
guide her back to her old home in the States; and when I
knew her, she was living under a large tree a few rods from
the rancho, and sleeping at night, with all her family, in
her one covered wagon. God only knows where they all
stowed themselves away, for she was a modern Mrs.

Rogers, with "nine small children and one at the breast;" indeed, of this catechismical number, the oldest was but fifteen years of age, and the youngest a nursing babe of six months. She had eight sons and one daughter. Just fancy how dreadful; only one girl to all that boy! People used to wonder what took me so often to her encampment, and at the interest with which I listened to what they called her "stupid talk." Certainly, there was nothing poetical about the woman. Leigh Hunt's friend could not have elevated *her* common-place into the sublime. She was immensely tall, and had a hard, weather-beaten face, surmounted by a dreadful horn comb and a heavy twist of hay-colored hair, which, before it was cut and its gloss all destroyed by the alkali, must, from its luxuriance, have been very handsome. But what interested me so much in her, was the dogged and determined way in which she had set that stern, wrinkled face of hers against poverty. She owned nothing in the world but her team, and yet she planned all sorts of successful ways, to get food for her small, or rather large family. She used to wash shirts, and iron them on a chair—in the open air, of course; and you can fancy with what success. But the gentlemen were too generous to be critical, and as they paid her three or four times as much as she asked, she accumulated quite a handsome sum in a few days. She made me think of a long-legged, very thin hen, scratching for dear life, to feed her never-to-be-satisfied brood. Poor woman! she told me that she seldom gave them as much as they could eat, at any one meal. She was worse off than the

———"old woman who lived in a shoe,
And had so many children she didn't know what to do;
To some she gave butter, and some she gave bread,
And to some she gave whippings, and sent them to bed."

Now *my* old woman had no butter and very little bread; and she was so naturally economical, that even whippings were sparingly administered. But after all their privations, they were—with the exception of the eldest hope—as healthy looking a set of ragged little wretches as ever I saw. The aforesaid "hope" was the longest, the leanest, and the bob-sidedest specimen of a Yankee that it is possible to imagine. He wore a white face, whiter eyes, and whitest hair; and walked about, looking as if existence was the merest burden, and he wished somebody would have the goodness to take it off his hands. He seemed always to be in the act of yoking up a pair of oxen, and ringing every change of which the English alphabet is capable, upon the one single Yankee execration, "*darnation!*" which he scattered, in all its comical varieties, upon the tow head of his young brother, a piece of chubby giggle, who was forever trying to hold up a dreadful yoke, which *wouldn't* "stay put," in spite of all the efforts of those fat, dirty little hands of his. The "long woman," mother like, excused him by saying that he had been sick; though once when the "darned fools" flew thicker than usual, she gently observed that "he had forgotten that he was a child himself once." He certainly retained no trace of having enjoyed that delightful state of existence; and though one would not be so rude as to call him an "old boy," yet being always clad in a middle-aged habit, an elderly coat and adult pantaloons, one would as little fancy him a *young* man. Perhaps the fact of his wearing his father's wardrobe, in all its unaltered amplitude, might help to confuse one's ideas on the subject.

There was another dear old lady, to whom I took the largest kind of liking, she was so exquisitely neat. Although she too had no floor, her babe always had on a clean white dress and face to match. She was about four feet high, and had a perfect passion for wearing those frightful frontpieces of false hair, with which the young women of L. were once in the habit of covering their abundant tresses. She used to send me little pots of fresh butter,—the first that I had tasted since I left the States,— beautifully stamped, and looking like ingots of virgin gold. I, of course, made a dead set at the frontpiece; though I do believe, that to this distorted taste, and its accompanying horror of a cap, she owed the preservation of her own beautiful hair. To please me she laid it aside; but I am convinced that it was restored to its proud eminence as soon as I left the valley, for she evidently had a "sneaking kindness" for it that nothing could destroy. I have sometimes thought that she wore it from religious principle, thinking it her duty to look as old as possible, for she appeared fifteen years younger when she took it off. She told me that in crossing the plains, she used to stop on Saturdays, and taking everything out of the wagons, wash them in strong lye; to which precaution she attributed the perfect health which they all enjoyed (the *family* not the wagons) during the whole journey.

There is one thing for which the immigrants deserve high praise, and that is, for having adopted the Bloomer dress, (frightful as it is on all other occasions) in crossing the plains. For such an excursion it is just the thing.

I ought to say a word about the dances which we used to have in the bar room, a place so low that a *very* tall man could not have stood upright in it. One side was fitted up as a store, and another side with bunks for lodgers. These bunks were elegantly draperied with red calico, through which we caught dim glimpses of blue blankets. If they could only have had sheets, they would have fairly been enveloped in the American colors. By the way, I wonder if there is anything *national* in this eternal passion for blue blankets and red calico? On ball nights the bar was closed, and everything was very quiet and respectable. To be sure, there was some danger of being swept away in a flood of tobacco juice; but luckily the floor was uneven, and it lay around in puddles, which with care one could avoid, merely running the minor risk of falling prostrate upon the wet boards, in the midst of a galopade.

Of course the company was made up principally of the immigrants. Such dancing, such dressing, and such conversation surely was never heard or seen before. The gentlemen, generally, were compelled to have a regular fight with their fair partners, before they could drag them on to the floor. I am happy to say, that almost always the stronger vessel won the day, or rather night, except in the case of certain timid youths, who after one or two attacks, gave up the battle in despair.

I thought that I had had some experience in bad grammar, since I came to California, but the good people were the first that I had ever heard use right royal *we*, instead of *us*. Do not imagine that all, or even the larger part of the company, were of this description. There were many intelligent and well-bred women, whose acquaintance I made with extreme pleasure.

After reading the description of the inconveniences and discomforts which we suffered in the American Valley,— and I can assure you that I have not at all exaggerated them,—you may imagine my joy when two of our friends arrived from Indian Bar, for the purpose of accompanying us home. We took two days for our return, and thus I was not at all fatigued. The weather was beautiful, our friends amusing, and F. well and happy. We stopped at night at a rancho, where they had a tame frog. You cannot think how comically it looked, hopping about the bar, quite as much at home as a tame squirrel would have been, I had a bed made up for me at this place, on one end of a long dining table. It was very comfortable, with the trifling drawback that I had to rise earlier than I wished, in order that what had been a bed at night, might become a table by day.

We stopped at the top of the hill, and set fire to some fir trees. Oh, how splendidly they looked, with the flames leaping and curling amid the dark green foliage, like a golden snake, fiercely beautiful. The shriek which the fire gave as it sprang upon its verdant prey, made me think of the hiss of some furious reptile, about to wrap in its burning folds its helpless victim.

With what perfect delight did I re-enter my beloved log cabin. One of our good neighbors had swept and put it in order before my arrival, and everything was clean and neat as possible. How gratefully to my feet felt the thick warm carpet; how perfect appeared the floor, which I had once reviled (I begged its pardon on the spot) because it was not exactly even; how cosy the old faded calico couch; how thoroughly comfortable the four chairs, (two of them had been thoroughly rebottomed with brown sail cloth, tastefully put on with a border of carpet tacks); how truly elegant the closet-case toilet table, with the doll's looking glass hanging above, which shewed my face—the first time that I had seen it since I left home—some six shades darker than usual; how convenient the trunk which did duty as a wash-stand, with its vegetable dish instead of a bowl, (at the rancho I had a pint tin pan, when it was not in use in the kitchen); but above and beyond all, how superbly luxurious the magnificent bedstead, with its splendid hair mattress, its clean wide linen sheets, its nice square pillows, and its large generous blankets and quilts. And then the cosy little supper, arrayed on a table-cloth; and the long, delightful evening afterwards, by a fragrant fire of beech and pine, when we talked over our past sufferings! Oh, it was delicious as a dream, and almost made amends for the three dreadful weeks of pleasuring in the American Valley.

LETTER TWENTY-THIRD

From our Log Cabin, Indian Bar,
Nov. 21, 1852

I SUPPOSE Molly, dear—at least, I flatter myself—that you have been wondering and fretting a good deal for the last few weeks, at not hearing from "Dame Shirley." The truth is, that I have been wondering and fretting *myself* almost into a fever, at the dreadful prospect of being compelled to spend the winter here, which, on every account, is undesirable.

To our unbounded surprise, we found, on our return from the American Valley, that nearly all the fluming companies had failed—contrary to every expectation, on arriving at the bed-rock, no gold made its appearance. But a short history of the rise, progress, and final fate of one of these associations, given me in writing by its own Secretary, conveys a pretty correct idea of the result of the majority of the remainder:

"The thirteen men, of which the 'American Fluming Company' consisted, commenced getting out timber in February. On the fifth of July, they began to lay the flume. A thousand dollars were paid for lumber, which they were compelled to buy. They built a dam six feet high and three hundred feet in length, upon which thirty men labored nine days and a half. The cost of said dam was estimated at two thousand dollars. This Company left off working on the twenty-fourth day of September, having taken out in *all*, gold dust to the amount of forty-one dollars and seventy cents! Their lumber and tools, sold at auction, brought about two hundred dollars."

A very small amount of arithmetical knowledge, will enable one to figure up what the "American Fluming Company" made, by *their* Summer's work. This result was, by no means, a singular one; nearly every person on the river received the same step-mother's treatment from Dame Nature, in this her mountain workshop.

Of course the whole world (*our* world,) was, to use a phrase much in vogue here, "dead broke." The shop-keepers, restaurants, and gambling houses, with an amiable confidingness peculiar to such people, had trusted the miners to that degree, that they themselves were in the same moneyless condition. Such a batch of woful faces was never seen before, not the least elongated of which, was F.'s—to whom nearly all the companies owed large sums.

Of course, with the failure of the golden harvest, "Othello's occupation was gone." The mass of the unfortunates laid down the "shovel and the hoe," and left the river in crowds. It is said, that there are not twenty men remaining on Indian Bar, although two months ago, you could count them up by hundreds.

We were to have departed on the fifth of November, and my toilet-table and wash-hand-stand, duly packed for that occasion—their occupation *also* gone—have remained ever since in the humble position of mere trunks. To be sure, the express-man called for us at the appointed time; but, unfortunately, F. had not returned from the American Valley, where he had gone to visit a sick friend, and Mr. Jones was not willing to wait even one day, so much did he fear being caught in a snow-storm with his mules. It was the general opinion, from unmistakable signs, that the rainy-season would set in a month earlier than common, and with unusual severity. Our friends urged me to start on with Mr. Jones, and some other acquaintances, and leave F. to follow on foot, as he could easily overtake us in a few hours. This I decidedly refused to do, preferring to run the fearful risk of being compelled to spend the Winter in the mountains, which—as there is not enough flour to last six weeks, and we, personally, have not laid in a pound of provisions—is not so indifferent a matter as it may at first appear to you. The traders have delayed getting in their Winter stock, on account of the high price of flour; and God only knows how fatal may be the result of this selfish delay to the unhappy mountaineer, many of whom having families here, are unable to escape into the valley.

It is the twenty-first day of November; and for the last three weeks, it has rained and snowed alternately, with now and then a fair day sandwiched between, for the express purpose, as it has seemed, of aggravating our misery. For after twelve hours of such sunshine, as only our own California can show, we were sure to be gratified by an exceedingly well got up tableau of the deluge, *without* that ark of safety—a mule team, which, sister Anna-like, we were ever straining our eyes to see descending the hill. "There, I hear a mule bell," would be the cry, at least a dozen times a day, when away we would all troop to the door, to behold nothing but great, brown raindrops rushing merrily downward, as if in mockery of our sufferings. Five times did the "Squire"—who has lived for some two or three years in the mountains, and is quite weather-wise —solemnly affirm, that the rain was over for the present, and five times did the storm-torrent of the next morning give our prophet the lie. In the meanwhile, we have been expecting each day the advent of a mule train. Now, the rumor goes that Clark's mules have arrived at Pleasant Valley; and now that Bob Lewis's train has reached the Wild Yankee's; or that Jones, with any quantity of animals and provisions, has been seen on the brow of the hill, and will probably get in by evening. Thus constantly "is alternating light and gloom," in a way that nearly drives me mad.

The few men that have remained on the Bar, have amused themselves by prosecuting one another right and left. The "Squire," bless his honest, lazy Leigh Hunt-ish face, comes out strong on these occasions. He has pronounced decisions, which, for legal acumen, brilliancy and acuteness, would make Daniel Webster, could he hear them, tear his hair to that extent—from sheer envy—that he would be compelled to have a wig ever after. But jesting apart, the "Squire's" course has been so fair, candid, and sensible, that he has won golden opinions from all; and were it not for his insufferable laziness and good-nature, he would have made a most excellent justice of the peace. The prosecuting party generally "gets judgment," which is about all he *does* get; though sometimes the constable is more fortunate, as happened to-day to our friend W., who, having been detained on the Bar by the rain, got himself sworn into the above office for the fun of the thing. He performs his duties with great delight, and is always accompanied by a guard of honor, consisting of the majority of the men remaining in the place. He entered the cabin about one hour ago, when the following spicy conversation took place between him and F., who happened to be the prosecutor in this day's proceedings:

"Well, old fellow, did you see Big Bill?" eagerly inquired F.

"Yes!" is the short and sullen reply.

"And what did you *get*?" continued his questioner.

"I got THIS!" savagely shouts the amateur constable, at the same time pointing with a grin of rage, to a huge swelling on his upper lip, gleaming with all the colors of the rainbow.

"What did you do then?" was the next, meek inquiry.

"Oh, I came away!" says our brave, young officer of justice. And indeed it would have been madness to have resisted this delightful "Big Bill," who stands six feet four inches in his stockings, with a corresponding amount of bone and muscle, and is a star of the first magnitude in the boxing circles. F. saved the creature's life last Winter, having watched with him three nights in succession. He refuses to pay his bill, "Cos he gin him *calumny*, and other pizen doctor's stuff!" Of course, poor W. got dreadfully laughed at; though I looked as solemn as possible, while I stayed him with cups of coffee, comforted him with beef-steaks and onions, and coaxed the wounded upper-lip with an infinite succession of little bits of brown paper drowned in brandy.

I wish that you could see *me* about these times. I am generally found seated on a segar-box in the chimney corner, my chin in my hand, rocking backwards and forwards (*weaving*, you used to call it,) in a despairing way, and now and then casting a picturesquely hopeless glance about our dilapidated cabin. Such a looking place as it is! Not having been repaired, the rain pouring down the outside of the chimney—which is inside of the house—has liquefied the mud, which now lies in spots all over the splendid tin mantle-piece, and festoons itself in graceful arabesques along the sides thereof. The lining overhead is dreadfully stained, the rose-garlanded hangings are faded and torn, the sofa-covering displays picturesque glimpses of hay, and the poor, old worn-out carpet is not enough to make india-rubbers desirable.

Sometimes I lounge forlornly to the window, and try to take a birds-eye view of "out-doors." First, now a large pile of gravel prevents me seeing anything else; but by dint of standing on tip-toe, I catch sight of a hundred other

large piles of gravel—Pelion upon Ossa like heaps of gigantic stones—excavations of fearful deepness, innumerable
tents, calico hovels, shingle palaces, *ramaras*, (pretty,
arbor-like places, composed of green boughs, and bapti-
zed with that sweet name,) half a dozen blue and red-
shirted miners, and one hatless *hombre*, in garments of the
airiest description, reclining gracefully at the entrance of
the Humboldt, in that transcendental state of intoxication, when a man is compelled to hold on to the earth for
fear of falling off. The whole Bar is thickly peppered with
empty bottles, oyster cans, sardine boxes, and brandied
fruit jars, the harsher outlines of which are softened off by
the thinnest possible coating of radiant snow. The river,
freed from its wooden flume prison, rolls gradually by.
The green and purple beauty of these majestic, old mountains, looks lovelier than ever, through its pearl-like net-
work of foaming streamlets, while, like an immense con-
cave of pure sapphire, without spot or speck, the wonderful and never-enough-to-be-talked-about sky of California, drops down upon the whole, its fathomless splendor.
The day happens to be the inner fold of one of the atmo-
spheric sandwiches, alluded to above. Had it been otherwise, I doubt whether I should have had spirit enough to
write to you.

    I have just been called from my letter, to look at a won-
derfully curious gold specimen. I will try to describe it to
you, and to convince you that I do not exaggerate its rare
beauty, I must inform you that two friends of ours, have
each offered a hundred dollars for it; and a blacksmith in
the place, a man utterly unimaginative, who would not
throw away a red cent on a *mere* fancy, has tried to purchase it for fifty dollars. I wish most earnestly that you
could see it. It is of unmixed gold, weighing about two
dollars and a half. Your first idea in looking at it, is, of an

exquisite little basket. There is a graceful cover, with its rounded nub at the top, the three finely carved sides—it is tri-formed—the little stand, upon which it sets, and the tiny clasp which fastens it. In detail, it is still more beautiful. On one side, you see a perfect W, each finely shaded bar of which, is fashioned with the nicest exactness. The second surface presents to view a Grecian profile, whose delicately cut features remind you of the serene beauty of an antique gem. It is surprising how much expression this face contains, which is enriched by an oval setting of delicate beading. A plain, triangular space of burnished gold, surrounded with bead-work, similar to that which outlines the profile, seems left on purpose for a name. The owner, who is a Frenchman, decidedly refuses to sell this gem, and you will probably never have an opportunity to see, that the same Being who has commanded the violet to be beautiful, can fashion the gold—crucibled into metallic purity, within the earth's dark heart—into shapes as lovely and curious.

To my extreme vexation, Ned, that jewel of cooks, and fiddlers, departed at the first approach of rain; since when, I have been obliged to take up the former delightful employment myself. Really, everybody ought to go to the mines, just to see how little it takes to make people comfortable in the world. My ordinary utensils consist of,— item, one iron dipper, which holds exactly three pints; item, one brass kettle of the same size; and, item, the gridiron, made out of an old shovel, which I described in a former letter. With these three assistants, I perform absolute wonders in the culinary way. Unfortunately, I am generally compelled to get three breakfasts, for sometimes the front-stick *will* break, and then down comes the brass kettle of potatoes, and the dipper of coffee, extinguishing the fire, spilling the breakfast, wetting the carpet,

scalding the dog, waking up F. from an eleven-o'clock-in-
the-day dream, and compelling poor me to get up a second
edition of my morning's work, on safer and more scientific principles.

At dinner time, some good natured friend carves the
beef at a stove outside, on condition that he may have a
plate, knife and fork at our table. So when the meal is
ready, I spread on the said table—which at other times
does duty as a China closet—a quarter of a sheet, which
with its three companion quarters, was sanctified and set
apart, when I first arrived here, for that sacred purpose. As
our guests generally amount to six or eight, we dispense
the three tea-spoons at the rate of one to every two or
three persons. All sorts of outlandish dishes serve as tea-
cups; among others, wine-glasses and tumblers—there are
always plenty of these in the mines—figure largely. Last
night, our company being larger than usual, one of our
friends was compelled to take his tea out of a soup-plate!
The same individual, not being able to find a seat, went
outside and brought in an empty gin-cask, upon which he
sat, sipping iron table-spoons-full of his tea, in great apparent glory and contentment.

F. has just entered, with the joyful news that the
express-man has arrived. He says that it will be impossible
for mule trains to get in for some time to come, even if the
storm is really over, which he does not believe. In many
places on the mountains, the snow is already five feet in
depth; although, he thinks that so many people are constantly leaving for the valley, that the path will be kept
open; so that I can make the journey with comparative
ease on his horse, which he has kindly offered to lend me,
volunteering to accompany F. and some others, who will
make their exodus at the same time, on foot. Of course I
shall be obliged to leave my trunks, merely taking a

change of linen in a carpetbag. We shall leave to-morrow, whether it rain or snow, for it would be madness to linger any longer.

My heart is heavy at the thought of departing forever from this place. I *like* this wild and barbarous life; I leave it with regret. The solemn fir trees, "whose slender tops *are* close against the sky" here, the watching hills, and the calmly beautiful river, seem to gaze sorrowfully at me, as I stand in the moon-lighted midnight, to bid them farewell. Beloved, unconventional wood-life; divine Nature, into whose benign eyes I never looked, whose many voices, gay and glad, I never heard, in the artificial heart of the busy world,—I quit your serene teachings for a restless and troubled future. Yes, Molly, smile if you will at my folly; but I go from the mountains with a deep heart sorrow. I look kindly to this existence, which to you seems so sordid and mean. Here, at least, I have been contented. The "thistle-seed," as you call me, sent abroad its roots right lovingly into this barren soil, and gained an unwonted strength in what seemed to you such unfavorable surroundings. You would hardly recognize the feeble and half-dying invalid, who drooped languidly out of sight, as night shut down between your straining gaze and the good ship Manilla, as she wafted her far away from her Atlantic home, in the person of your *now* perfectly healthy sister.

SUGGESTED READINGS

Buck, Franklin A., *A Yankee Trader in the Gold Rush* (Boston, 1930)

Buffum, E. Gould, *Six Months in the Gold Mines* (Phila., 1850)

Caughey, John, *Gold is the Cornerstone* (Berkeley, 1948)

Colton, Walter, *Three Years in California* (New York, 1850)

Dane, G. Ezra, *Ghost Towns* (New York, 1941)

Delano, Alonzo, *Life on the Plains and Among the Diggings* (New York, 1854)

Jackson, Joseph H., *Gold Rush Album* (New York, 1949)

Lewis, Oscar, *Sea Routes to the Gold Fields* (New York, 1949)

Margo, Elizabeth, *Taming the Forty-Niner* (New York, 1955)

Marryat, Frank, *Mountains and Molehills* (London, 1855)

Paul, Rodman, *California Gold* (Cambridge, 1947)

Read, Georgia and Ruth Gaines, Eds., *Gold Rush: The Journals, Drawings, and Other Papers of J. Goldsborough Bruff* (New York, 1944)

Shinn, Charles H., *Mining Camps* (New York, 1885)

Taylor, Bayard, *El Dorado, or Adventures in the Path of Empire* (New York, 1850)

Wheat, Carl I., *Books of the California Gold Rush* (San Francisco, 1949)